Terence Ra

HARLEQUINADE
and
ALL ON HER OWN

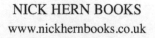
www.nickhernbooks.co.uk

www.branaghtheatre.com

A Nick Hern Book

This edition of *Harlequinade* and *All On Her Own* first published in Great Britain in 2015 as a paperback original by Nick Hern Books Limited, The Glasshouse, 49a Goldhawk Road, London W12 8QP, in association with the Kenneth Branagh Theatre Company. *Harlequinade* was first published in 1953 by Hamish Hamilton Ltd. *All On Her Own* was first published as *Duologue* in 2011 by Nick Hern Books.

Designed and typeset by Nick Hern Books, London
Printed in the UK by CPI Group (UK) Ltd

A CIP catalogue record for this book is available from the British Library

ISBN 978 1 84842 541 5

Contents

Introduction by Michael Darlow   v

Production Details   xii

Interview with Kenneth Branagh and Rob Ashford   xv

Interview with Zoë Wanamaker   xix

Interview with Christopher Oram   xxii

Harlequinade   1

All On Her Own   59

Introduction
Michael Darlow

These two one-act plays, produced as a double bill in the Kenneth Branagh Theatre Company's 2015–16 season at London's Garrick Theatre, were written on either side of the great divide in Terence Rattigan's career. *Harlequinade* was first produced in 1948, when Rattigan was widely regarded as Britain's finest practising playwright; *All On Her Own* was written in 1968, the period when his critical reputation was at its lowest.

The contrast between the two plays could not be greater either. *All On Her Own* is about love and the need to feel needed, the subject to which Rattigan returned repeatedly. *Harlequinade*, which Rattigan described as 'a farce of character', is about Rattigan's greatest love of all – the theatre.

Rattigan was born in South Kensington on 10th June 1911, the second son of the troubled marriage of Frank, a rising young diplomat, and Vera, a strong-minded Edwardian beauty. Because of his parents' prolonged postings overseas, for much of his early life he was left in the care of a grandmother, becoming increasingly unhappy and withdrawn. Family friends came to refer to him as 'That poor lost child, Terry Rattigan'.

He was first taken to the theatre by an aunt when he was about seven. The play was *Cinderella*, and he was completely captivated: 'I believed in everything I saw on that stage… it was important to me that Cinderella should go to the ball and marry the prince.' From that moment he became determined to become a playwright.

In 1933, while he was at Oxford, a play he had written with a fellow undergraduate, *First Episode*, was produced at a small theatre in Kew. With its depiction of Oxford student life – drunken parties, gambling, casual sex – it provoked a small sensation and was transferred into the West End. Buoyed up by this brush with success, Rattigan left Oxford without taking a degree and moved into a London flat to embark on a career as a dramatist. But just weeks later the play closed. Broke, Rattigan was forced to return home and throw himself on his parents' mercy.

Although displeased by his son's precipitate decision to leave Oxford without a degree, his father agreed to pay him a small allowance to stay at home and write plays on condition that if, after two years, he had not succeeded as a playwright he would take whatever job could be found for him.

For the next two years Rattigan wrote play after play but each one was rejected. So, with the two years up, he took a lowly hack job as a member of a team of writers kept on the payroll at Warner Brothers Studios in Teddington to write additional lines of dialogue for whatever film was in production at the studios. Then, just weeks later, his luck changed. In November 1936 one of his previously rejected comedies, *French Without Tears*, was rushed into production as a stopgap at the Criterion Theatre. It was a surprise smash-hit. It ran for over 1,000 performances and made Rattigan and its young cast, including Rex Harrison, Trevor Howard and Roland Culver, famous.

This sudden success after the years of rejection caused a reaction which Rattigan later described as a nervous breakdown. In the next six years he completed just two plays: *Follow My Leader* – co-written with a friend from Oxford, a satire on Hitler and the British policy of appeasement, which was banned by the Lord Chamberlain on the grounds that it might offend Hitler – and a drama, *After the Dance*, which opened in June 1939 to good notices but, with the approach of war, closed after just sixty performances.

Advised by a psychiatrist to join up and experience active service, Rattigan became an air gunner in RAF Coastal Command. The fierce concentration, shared danger and camaraderie of life in the RAF cured Rattigan's 'writer's block' and, writing in his off-duty hours, hit after hit flowed from his pen – *Flare Path* (1942), *While the Sun Shines* (1943), *Love in Idleness* (1944), *The Winslow Boy* (1946), plus the scripts for five well-received films. In 1948 came *Playbill*, two one-act plays – *The Browning Version* and *Harlequinade*. More successes followed, including *The Deep Blue Sea* (1952) and *Separate Tables* (1954). However, by the 1950s this almost unfailing run of successes had begun to make Rattigan suspect. Surely, no playwright who was as consistently successful as he was could really be that good? A repertory theatre manager told him: 'We so like putting on your plays here, Mr Rattigan. They pay for the good ones.'

By 1956, with the arrival of a new, younger generation, the start of the English Stage Company at the Royal Court and John Osborne's *Look Back in Anger*, followed by Brendan Behan's *The Quare Fellow* at Joan Littlewood's Theatre Workshop and the first visit to London of the Berliner Ensemble with plays by Bertolt Brecht, Rattigan's reputation had undergone a complete sea change. Now he was seen as the standard bearer for an old, out-of-touch theatre, cut off from the realities of most ordinary people's lives. Despite his unfailingly calm and unruffled demeanour, Rattigan had always suffered from a deep lack of self-confidence and became hugely discouraged. In the remaining twenty-one years of his life he wrote just five plays and another one-act double bill. Most of his time was given over to writing highly paid Hollywood films. His reputation only started to recover towards the end of his life and it was not until his centenary in 2011, with the dozens of revivals of his plays, seasons of his films, exhibitions, TV programmes and articles, that his qualities came to be fully recognised.

All On Her Own was the result of a 1968 BBC2 Television commission to thirteen well-known writers (others included J.B. Priestley, John Mortimer and Emlyn Williams) to write a short solo play for an actress of their choice. It owes much to Rattigan's own experience and his reassessment of his parents' relationship. For most of his adult life Rattigan had blamed his father for the difficulties in his parents' marriage – his numerous affairs and often boorish attitude to his mother's interests. But by 1967, when he started work on the play, his father was dead and his mother had become an increasingly difficult and self-centred old lady, and Rattigan had begun to suspect that the problems in the marriage had also been down to his mother; to her unbending attitudes, her buttoned-up views on sex and her unconcealed disappointment with her husband over his failed career as a diplomat – he had been forced to 'retire early' from the diplomatic service following a row with the Foreign Secretary, Lord Curzon, over British policy towards Turkey. The play can be seen as, in part, a portrait of his mother. But the woman in the play, Rosemary, can also be seen as a self-portrait of Rattigan himself. He, like Rosemary, was always 'impeccably polite'. He hated rows and unpleasantness, even letting people steal from him rather than confront them. Rosemary, like Rattigan, has a deep-seated need to feel needed, a need which, in Rattigan's case, probably had its origins in his childhood.

Harlequinade was intended as 'the lightest soufflé' to balance the serious drama *The Browning Version* in his 1948 double bill, *Playbill*. But it too touches on Rattigan's deepest concerns and draws upon important events in own his life. In it a star husband and wife, Arthur and Edna Gosport, are dress-rehearsing a revival of their production of *Romeo and Juliet* in a theatre somewhere in the Midlands. In 1932, while at Oxford, Rattigan had been in a prestigious Oxford University Dramatic Society production of *Romeo and Juliet*, directed by John Gielgud. Rattigan had one line as one of the musicians who discover Juliet's body: 'Faith, we may put up our pipes and be gone.' On the first night all was going well until late in the play when Rattigan played his one line. Because of the way he played it, the audience, instead of sitting frozen in suspense, roared with laughter. At each succeeding performance Rattigan tried to kill the laugh by saying the line with a different inflection but to steadily worsening effect, until the last performance when he spoke the line so quietly that no one heard it. This incident is drawn upon directly in the play. In his creation of the character of Arthur Gosport, his mannerisms, the way he conducts the rehearsal, his bounding enthusiasm, absent-mindedness and total absorption in the production to the exclusion of all else, Rattigan draws heavily on his memories of watching Gielgud at Oxford.

Another important influence was Rattigan's experience in 1944 of working with Alfred Lunt and his wife Lynn Fontanne, on *Love in Idleness*, in which they played a couple living 'in sin'. Rattigan wrote to his mother: 'The atmosphere in rehearsals in which we are all living is apparently the only atmosphere in which they can work happily. It is, however, reminiscent of John Gielgud, only worse, because there are two of them.' He describes how they remain totally charming towards each other even when they are disagreeing over a bit of business or the way a line should be played, while at the same time trying to get their own way.

In the years immediately after the war, when Rattigan was working on *Harlequinade*, there was a vogue for plays in verse, many with religious themes, written in language that often seemed deliberately impenetrable. The playwrights involved probably believed that they were following in the footsteps of T.S. Eliot, Auden and Isherwood, but unfortunately they had nothing like their talent. One particularly ripe example, which is alluded to in *Harlequinade*, is Ronald Duncan's 1946 play *This Way to the Tomb*.

1946, the year in which Rattigan started working on *Harlequinade*, was the year in which the National Health Service Act and the new National Insurance Act were passed. It was also the year in which the Arts Council came into being, described by John Maynard Keynes, the principal force behind its creation, as: 'The spiritual wing of the Welfare State, tending to the nation's psychic health as the NHS will tend to its physical health.' Direct government funding of the arts had begun during the war with the creation of CEMA (the Committee for the Encouragement of Music and the Arts) with the aim of improving the morale of the population and promoting British culture and the values for which we were fighting. CEMA funded companies of actors, singers and dancers to perform major modern and classic plays in towns and cities around the country to audiences, many of whom had never been to the theatre before. The Old Vic relocated from London to the Grand Theatre in Burnley from where it sent out tours, led by great actors such as husband and wife Sybil Thorndike and Lewis

Casson, to play Shakespeare in Welsh mining villages and the industrial towns of the north. Among other, rather less accomplished, companies led by star husband-and-wife teams which received CEMA and, later, Arts Council funding to tour the classics around industrial areas previously deprived of the arts, was one led by Donald Wolfit and his wife Rosalind Iden. Wolfit was widely accused of being vain and of hiring inferior actors so as to ensure that he and his wife remained the centre of the audience's attention, outshining those on stage around them. 1946 was also the year in which the Arts Council arranged for a company from the Old Vic to take over the running of the Theatre Royal in Bristol, thus creating the Bristol Old Vic.

The views expressed by Edna Selby and Jack, the stage manager, about the Arts Council and its policies are similar to those expressed by many older actors of the period and, in some respects, not unlike those of Rattigan himself. He put similar views into the mouth of 'Aunt Edna', a character he invented for the Introduction to Volume II of his *Collected Plays* in 1953, to defend his plays from the charge that because they were popular they could not be any good. Aunt Edna is, in many ways, remarkably like Rattigan's mother, Vera. She is the unchanging theatregoer down the ages, from the Greek theatre of Sophocles, through the age of Shakespeare to the London theatre of Rattigan's day. She does not know a great deal about the theatre, but she knows what she likes and over time, Rattigan claims, her tastes have proved an infallible barometer of what is really good and what is merely fashionable, of which plays will endure and which will not. She has strong views about the other arts as well, views similar to those expressed by Rosemary in *All On Her Own*.

Both *All On Her Own* and *Harlequinade*, as well as touching on relationships, issues and events of great importance to Rattigan himself, also explore concerns which remain of importance to today's audience. Today, with our increased life expectancy, far higher incidence of relationship breakdown and of single older people living alone, Rosemary, a widow living alone, is an even more familiar figure than she would have been to audiences in the 1960s when Rattigan wrote the play.

Similarly, today the whole issue of government and local-authority funding for the arts and culture, the purpose and promised social and cultural value of such funding and the policies of the Arts Council (which are central to the putting on of the Gosports' production of *Romeo and Juliet*, around which the action in *Harlequinade* revolves) are again very much 'under the spotlight'. But whereas in the 1940s, when Rattigan wrote *Harlequinade*, the focus was on the steadily increasing amounts being spent on arts funding and the growing range of cultural initiatives involved, today the focus is on repeated cuts in government and local-authority spending on the arts and the diminishing range and scope of those activities. Nevertheless, no matter what the political climate or changing fashions in acting and production, the whole, often messy and sometimes chaotic, business of putting on a play remains timeless, essentially the same now as it was in Rattigan's day, in the age of Shakespeare or in ancient Athens.

Neither *All On Her Own* nor *Harlequinade* may rank among the greatest works in the Rattigan canon, but they remain highly pertinent and relevant for a modern audience. Together they offer a valuable insight into Rattigan's enduring strengths – his deep understanding of the human heart, his sure touch with comedy and his deep love for the theatre.

Michael Darlow's biography Terence Rattigan: The Man and His Work *is published by Quartet Books*.

This double bill of *Harlequinade* and *All On Her Own* was first performed as part of the Kenneth Branagh Theatre Company's Plays at the Garrick season, at the Garrick Theatre, London, on 7 November 2015 (previews from 24 October), with the following cast:

HARLEQUINADE

SECOND HALBERDIER	Jaygann Ayeh
JACK WAKEFIELD	Tom Bateman
ARTHUR GOSPORT	Kenneth Branagh
MURIEL PALMER	Jessie Buckley
MISS FISHLOCK	Vera Chok
TOM PALMER	Jack Colgrave Hirst
POLICEMAN	John Dagleish
FIRST HALBERDIER	Hadley Fraser
JOHNNY	Ansu Kabia
FRED INGRAM	Stuart Neal
WARDROBE MISTRESS	Zoë Rainey
EDNA SELBY	Miranda Raison
REHEARSAL PIANIST	Michael Rouse
GEORGE CHUDLEIGH	John Shrapnel
DAME MAUD	Zoë Wanamaker
JOYCE LANGLAND	Kathryn Wilder
MR BURTON	Jimmy Yuill

ALL ON HER OWN

ROSEMARY HODGE	Zoë Wanamaker

Director	Rob Ashford
Director	Kenneth Branagh
Set and Costume Designer	Christopher Oram
Lighting Designer	Neil Austin
Sound Designer	Christopher Shutt
Composer	Patrick Doyle
Projection Designer	Jon Driscoll
Casting Director	Lucy Bevan
Wigs, Hair and Make-up	Carol Hemming
Resident Director	Nicola Samer
Voice Consultant	Barbara Houseman
Fight Director	Bret Yount
Set and Costume Design Assistant	Frankie Bradshaw
Casting Associate	Emily Brockmann

PRODUCERS

For The Kenneth Branagh Theatre Company
Kenneth Branagh
Tamar Thomas

For Fiery Angel
Edward Snape
Marilyn Eardley

General Manager for Fiery Angel
Jon Bath

ARTISTIC ASSOCIATES

Rob Ashford
Christopher Oram

COMPANY

Production Manager	Jim Leaver
Costume Supervisor	Mary Charlton
Props Supervisor	Celia Strainge
Wigs Supervisor	Richard Mawbey
Company Manager	Gemma Tonge
Stage Manager	Tanya Gosling
Deputy Stage Managers	Fran O'Donnell
	Rhiannon Harper
Assistant Stage Managers	Stuart Campbell
	Sarah Coates
	Emily Hardy
Head of Wardrobe	Tim Gradwell
Wardrobe Deputy	Rachael McIntyre
Wardrobe Assistant	Rosie Etheridge
Head of Wigs	Gemma Flaherty
Head of Sound	Wayne Harris
Music Director	Patrick Neil Doyle
Music Supervisor	Maggie Rodford
Music Programmer	Rupert Cross
Lighting Programmer	Rob Halliday
Production Electrician	Martin Chisnall
Production Carpenter	Martin Riley
Dressers	Jenni Carvell
	Spencer Kitchen
Associate Costume Supervisor	Kitty Hawkins
Assistant Props Supervisor	Abby Price
Production Coordinator	Sarah Sweeney
Production Associate	Nick Morrison
Assistant to Kenneth Branagh	Max Gill

Kenneth Branagh and Rob Ashford, co-directors
Speaking to Nicola Samer and Max Gill

This season marks the reunion of your artistic collaboration. How do you negotiate this creative relationship?

KB We talk as often as possible. And as early as possible.

RA I would say to obviously make sure that we're both on the same page.

KB Early exchange of information. When we have an idea we share it in person, with a phone call, via email. And sometimes years ahead. First conversations are had as soon as we read the play. We're often creatures of instinct. I had an instinct that, should the Estate be sympathetic to it, Rattigan's own questioning of how *Harlequinade* should end might be met with the right kind of song. I put this to Rob over many months of deliberation and he came up with what I thought was the perfect song for our answer, so it's that kind of thing. We try to keep as many positive question marks going as we can.

Harlequinade *was originally in a double bill with* The Browning Version. *How do you think it communicates with* All On Her Own, *if at all?*

KB I think that always, Rattigan seems to be writing secretly within a play that appears to be promising something different. Everything about his life seems to have an element of disguise; his background, his accent, his sexual life. In *Harlequinade*, he seems unable to write merely a farce. It ends up being quite interested in familial relationships, paternal rejection, and the perils of being a kind of orphan. His first title for *Harlequinade* was *Perdita*. Nor can he, in *All On Her Own*, merely write a

'Hampstead lady' of the kind that people might expect from him. He ends up unleashing the fathom-full depths of a human being. Rosemary comes from a particular social strata, but Rattigan's interest is in seeing what lies far beneath the surface.

RA In *Harlequinade*, I think it's also interesting that Rattigan included the character of Joyce, Jack's fiancée, who appears to be more of a typical Rattigan character. I think it is a lovely moment, at just the right time, when Joyce shows up. In a way it reminds us of what Rattigan usually writes. I think that's very clever of him.

What is the appeal of Rattigan for a modern audience?

KB He has great intelligence, wit and emotion. A dynamite combination.

RA Vulnerability in the characters. Vulnerability in whatever situation they're in.

KB A good story, strongly told. He encourages people to be on the edge of their seats, wondering what will happen next.

RA A lot of unfolding moments of drama.

KB He's effortlessly witty. And I think people have begun to understand that he's also genuinely multilayered and complex. They look for that surprise; they come to know and warmly appreciate that he is interested in dissecting what lies beneath smooth surfaces.

RA That's right. They look underneath through what's on top.

How have you approached the balance of comedy and human drama in Harlequinade?

RA I think the main thing that we've discovered is that there must be a humanness in it. The characters and situations are so well written that the way we seem to have found more humour in the play is by playing the truth more. We play the truth more and somehow that actually brings out the humour.

KB Rattigan is a playwright, like Shakespeare, of great range. He understands the value of contrast, comedy and drama inside the same play, or even the same scene, being obvious examples.

The best comedy is often punctuated with moments of darkness. Where can we find this chiaroscuro in Rattigan's work?

KB Secrets. He's interested in secrets. People with pasts. Many of the plays are quite Wildean in that way. In both these plays there is a big question mark about what the truth of the past-uncovered will reveal. Will it transform or destroy the lives of those who experience it in the present? He plays that for the suspense and the drama but he gives the chance for it to have an emotional and sometimes humorous catharsis.

RA And he doesn't tie it up with a bow either. It's not all concluded at the end. Sad or happy. It's left open. It's left to continue in your mind as you leave with a lot questions.

Harlequinade *is about a very specific era in Britain's theatrical history. Has anything surprised you in your preparation and rehearsal for the play?*

KB I think there's a universality about the heightened atmosphere of what can be a certain semi-hysteria when a live performance is under pressure of deadline and time. It seemed there was a personal connection with Rattigan's own experience of being the Halberdier who has to say 'Faith we may put up our pipes and begone' in John Gielgud's production of *Romeo and Juliet* that both amused and haunted him. Even though it's from a particular period, the would-be follies, and sometimes very poignant experiences of 'showbiz folk' are made universal and timeless by Rattigan's touch, despite being rooted just after the war.

RA I've just been so fascinated, working on *The Winter's Tale* and *Harlequinade* at the same time, of the parallel story of a lost daughter, the finding of her, and what that means to both these men [Leontes and Arthur Gosport]. I think it's extremely powerful and I see it throughout the plays so much. I do think that in this production of *Harlequinade*, because we are doing *The Winter's Tale* at the same time, this story of the lost and found daughter is so beautiful. Something about that connection between those two people in *Harlequinade* actually lifts the humour all around it. That moment of the play is really going to be lifted up with *The Winter's Tale* playing on other nights.

The season has an emphasis on the importance of company. Why is this important to you both and why now?

KB When you do several plays together, I think there is an interchange of ideas and support. There's a dialogue between more and less experienced people. You have more hands on deck to do the work. You have more examples and inspirations of how the work might be achieved technically, or how difficult language might be spoken naturally. There is a passing of that knowledge around. There's a sense of event. There's a sense of collaboration that's different from performing a one-off play. There's a kind of transparency about how things are done. When the goal is the pursuit of excellence and you are working on the plays of very fine writers, a high level of skill needs to be acquired and that needs to be gathered in a specialist group.

RA I also think that when doing three plays at once, there's a triple commitment to working together and creating together.

Zoë Wanamaker,
Dame Maud in *Harlequinade* **and Rosemary Hodge in**
All On Her Own
Speaking to Nicola Samer and Max Gill

What attracted you to the part of Rosemary Hodge in All On
Her Own*?*

I found the play intriguing. It could go anywhere, it could be
done as a dance piece, it could be done with all the access that
theatre provides, in the way of sound, visuals, lighting and
movement. It even has a mime element to it. When I first read it
I saw it as a film noir. Something that could have been made by
Buñuel or Fellini. It is a very mercurial piece.

What is your approach to creating character?

A lot of it is instinct and imaginative work, but there are
questions that I have always asked which are:

What is the play about?

Why did the writer write the play?

What does the director want to say about the play?

If you took your character out of the play, what would happen
to the play?

Those are the main questions I always ask and those are the
fundamentals from where I come from. I have quite a visual
mind; in my head I can work out a backstory, the way I think it
should look, and the impression that I would like the play to give.

I do a lot of research, reading, looking at paintings, listening to
music of the time and then it all goes into the work and the

rehearsal period. I don't write things down very much but I know I have them in my head. I have worked out, for instance, where Rosemary was brought up, the before and after of the play. This is how I approach every job that I do.

Can you discuss your visual diary, which you shared with us during rehearsals, in greater detail?

It kicked off when Ken gave me my copy of the script, which had three images on the front of it, which puzzled me. It prompted me to find my own images of how I felt.

These included Magritte, Picasso, Matisse, Horst, Munch, Stezaker and Alex Katz and many more. I have added to the diary throughout rehearsals as I kept finding more images that reflected my emotions about the piece.

What do you think draws audiences to Rattigan's writing?

His plays have a somewhat Chekhovian feeling about them. The undertones of the characters are very strong, which is of course also very English in the sense that what's underneath is as important as what they say. For me, Terence Rattigan is about suppressed emotion.

Freud characterises guilt as a kind of 'moral masochism'. Do you think this is a fair appraisal of Rosemary's situation?

Yes, to some extent I think that's true of Rosemary. The psychological reading around the subject that I've done has also been about the process of grieving. When somebody loses someone, guilt and grief can often collude, which is to some extent what Freud is talking about. At the same time, every theory has a spin-off, although I think that's not a bad one.

Harlequinade *focuses on a touring theatre company. How have
your own experiences informed how you have approached
Dame Maud?*

Only slightly. I think the days when I was touring were very
different, but there is that element of knowing that you have to
fix up your digs, where you stayed for the week, how you
arranged yourself. What we're talking about [in terms of
working conditions for touring companies] in the time of play
following the war was much more basic and frugal. My
repertory days were a little bit more civilized in comparison, I
would imagine.

What do you hope audiences will take away with them from All
On Her Own?

Oh gosh, I have no idea! I hope that they feel as intrigued about
the piece as I do. It's a privilege to be able to present it in the
West End and to a wider audience.

*What have you learnt that surprised you during the rehearsal
process?*

The play surprised me when I first performed it all in one. To
find the emotional route of both characters is what I have found
most difficult to achieve. What I find very difficult is to run it as
a piece, but I'm sure that this will become easier the more I run
it with an audience. I have to be very sure about the steps that I
do in order for the emotional tension to be released; I have to
have a map like a piece of choreography. Until I have that route
map, I'm constantly checking that I'm doing the right thing. I
feel the energy to run it is too much sometimes, and I find it
very threatening and challenging. I'm not good at letting go of
my emotions unless I'm absolutely secure in what I'm doing. I
am very self-critical, like most actors, and a very good judge of
when I'm lying.

Christopher Oram, designer
Speaking to Nick Morrison

Tell us about your process – where do you begin to work on a project?

I always start with the text. Serving the writer is always my chief intention. I respect the writer above all, as it from his or her imagination that we all draw inspiration, and in Shakespeare and Rattigan we have two unquestionable masters of the form, so where better to start?

Is working on plays in rep very different to working on 'normal' shows?

Everything changes. It is an entirely different, fantastically more complicated, expensive and challenging process. Some buildings are designed for, while others can at least lend themselves better to, the rep process, but unfortunately the Garrick is not one of those. A beautiful intimate playhouse, it however has a relatively small raked stage with very little wing space (for storage), and very limited flying capacity. So the challenge of squeezing not one, not two, but three shows into the same space at the same time was a particularly singular (albeit in triplicate) process...

When do you start to work on a model box?

As soon as I can! The design process tends to extend and contract to suit the amount of time one has to do it in! But as this project has been constantly changing and evolving, not least when the one show became two, then three, this has been a particularly extended, but ultimately rewarding, adventure.

Given that Harlequinade *is a play about theatre, what sort of references did you look for in this production?*

The meta nature of putting on a play about putting on a play, led by an actor-manager, here in 2015 by a new company in the West End, led by a modern-day actor-manager is almost enough to blow your mind, but it was really fun to get inside the process of designing the show within the show. To design a show as it might have been designed seventy years ago alongside our contemporary production of *The Winter's Tale* was a satisfying juxtaposition of styles and ideas, made all the more meta of course by the knowledge that we are going to be doing our own production of *Romeo and Juliet* later in year.

What were the big decisions you had to make in costuming the show?

To have as much fun as possible, but remain truthful, to our actors, to their characters, and to the writer's intention for them and for the piece.

Harlequinade model box

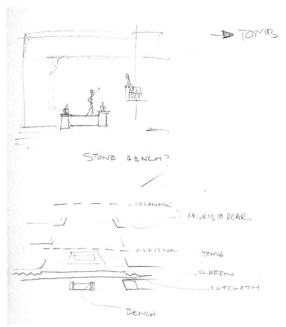

Early *Harlequinade* sketch

Balcony sketch

Zoë Wanamaker as Dame Maud

Zoë Wanamaker as the Nurse

HARLEQUINADE

Terence Rattigan

Harlequinade was first produced in a double bill with *The Browning Version*, under the joint title *Playbill*, at the Phoenix Theatre, London, on 8 September 1948, with the following cast:

ARTHUR GOSPORT	Eric Portman
EDNA SELBY	Mary Ellis
DAME MAUD GOSPORT	Marie Löhr
JACK WAKEFIELD	Hector Ross
GEORGE CHUDLEIGH	Kenneth Edwards
FIRST HALBERDIER	Peter Scott
SECOND HALBERDIER	Basil Howes
MISS FISHLOCK	Noel Dyson
FRED INGRAM	Anthony Oliver
JOHNNY	Henry Bryce
MURIEL PALMER	Thelma Ruby
TOM PALMER	Patrick Jordan
MR BURTON	Campbell Cotts
JOYCE LANGLAND	Henryetta Edwards
POLICEMAN	Manville Tarrant
Director	Peter Glenville

Foreword to Mr Wilmot

You and I both know, dear Mr Wilmot – who better? – that if the correct definition of farce is 'the theatrical presentation of unlikely events' then this play belies its label. I freely admit, dear Mr Wilmot, that, in calling it a farce I am most grossly deceiving that great and innocent Public who know so much about Life and so little about the Theatre. For this misnomer, therefore, I beg, dear Mr Wilmot, your gracious forgiveness. For you, I know, would more properly be inclined to call it tragedy; so, too, in all probability, the critics; and so too, perhaps, even that great and still innocent Public who know so much about the Theatre and so little about Life; while I, myself, would indeed agree with you all did not the claim of decorum, to which you, dear Mr Wilmot, should ever lend as lively an ear as myself, demand that I continue to call this play what it palpably is not – to wit, a farce.

Characters

ARTHUR GOSPORT
EDNA SELBY
DAME MAUD GOSPORT
JACK WAKEFIELD
GEORGE CHUDLEIGH
FIRST HALBERDIER
SECOND HALBERDIER
MISS FISHLOCK
FRED INGRAM
JOHNNY
MURIEL PALMER
TOM PALMER
MR BURTON
JOYCE LANGLAND
POLICEMAN

Setting

The stage of a theatre in a Midlands town.

Harlequinade

*Scene: the stage of a theatre in a Midlands town. The lights are
out on the rise of the curtain. They come on gradually to reveal
the graceful figure of* ARTHUR GOSPORT *as he enters. He is
dressed in doublet and tights.*

ARTHUR (*shouting over his shoulder*). He jests at scars that
    never felt a wound.

    *The lights now reveal enough for us to see that he has found
    himself in an unmistakable, if rather severely functional,
    fifteenth-century Italian garden, with, at one side, the
    balcony of a house, from the window of which is shining a
    light.*

    But, soft! What light through yonder window breaks?
    It is the east, and Juliet is the sun!
    Arise, fair sun, and kill the envious moon,
    Who is already sick and pale with grief,
    That thou her maid art far more fair than she:
    Be not her maid, since she is envious;
    Her vestal livery is but sick and green,
    And none but fools do wear it; cast it off.

    Juliet, in the person of EDNA SELBY, *appears at the
    balcony above.*

    It is my lady; O, it is my love!
    O, that she knew she were!

    EDNA *emits a melodious sigh and gives a sad shake of the
    head.*

    She speaks, yet she says nothing; and what of that?
    Her eye discourses, I will answer it.

    He comes forward, then leaps back.

    I am too bold, 'tis not to me she speaks:
    Two of the fairest stars in all the heaven,

Having some business, do entreat her eyes
To twinkle in their spheres till they return.
What if her eyes were there, they in her head?
The brightness of her cheek would shame those stars,
As daylight doth a lamp; her eyes in heaven
Would through the airy region stream so bright
That birds would sing, and think it were not night.

EDNA *emits another melodious sigh, and rests her cheek thoughtfully upon her hand.*

See how she leans her cheek upon her hand!
O, that I were a glove upon that hand,
That I might touch that cheek!

EDNA. Ah me!

ARTHUR.   She speaks:
O, speak again, bright angel! for thou art
As glorious to this night, being o'er my head,
As is a winged messenger of heaven
Unto the white-upturned wondering eyes
Of mortals that fall back to gaze on him
When he bestrides the lazy-pacing clouds
And sails upon the bosom of the air.

EDNA. O Romeo, Romeo! Wherefore art thou Romeo?
Deny thy father and refuse thy name;
Or, if thou wilt not, be but sworn my love,
And I'll no longer be a Capulet.

ARTHUR (*aside*). Shall I hear more, or shall I speak at this?

In the intense excitement of his passion he gives a boyish leap onto a garden stool. EDNA's glance momentarily wavers from the upper regions of the theatre, on which her eyes have been sentimentally fixed since the beginning of the scene.

EDNA. 'Tis but thy name that is my enemy;
Thou art thyself though, not a Montague.
What's Montague?

Darling, are you going to do that tonight?

ARTHUR. What?

EDNA. That little jump.

ARTHUR. Well – yes – I thought I would. Why? Does it bother you?

EDNA. No, darling. Just so long as I know, that's all.

ARTHUR. Sorry, darling. That's quite all right. Let's go back. (*To prompt corner.*) Yes?

JOHNNY (*from prompt corner*). 'Tis but thy name –

EDNA (*sharply*). No. Before that. I want to give Mr Gosport the cue for his little jump.

JOHNNY (*off*). What little jump, Miss Selby?

EDNA. The little jump he does onto that stool.

Enter JOHNNY.

JOHNNY. Mr Gosport doesn't do a little jump, Miss Selby.

EDNA. Yes, he does do a little jump. He's just done a little jump.

JOHNNY. He's never done a little jump before.

EDNA. I know he's never done a little jump before. But he's doing a little jump now. He's just put a little jump in.

ARTHUR. Look – I don't think I'll do the little jump, after all.

EDNA. Yes, you shall, my darling. You shall do the little jump. It looked very charming – very youthful. (*To prompt corner.*) When Mr Gosport says: 'Shall I speak at this?' he does a little jump onto a stool. Now what's my line before that?

JOHNNY (*going off*). And I'll no longer be a Capulet.

EDNA (*resuming her pose*).
Or, if thou wilt not, be but sworn my love,
And I'll no longer be a Capulet.

ARTHUR *does his leap again, only this time it is, perhaps, not quite so boyish as before.*

ARTHUR. Shall I hear more or shall I speak at this?

EDNA. 'Tis but thy name that is my enemy;
Thou art thyself though, not a Montague.
What's Montague?

*While speaking she has appeared to be struggling to keep
her composure. She now loses the battle and laughs outright.*

Sorry, darling.

ARTHUR. Does it look awfully silly? I won't do it, then.

EDNA. Oh no – you must do it. Come on. Let's try again.

ARTHUR. No. I won't do it if it's as funny as all that. I only
thought it might help the boyishness of the line, that's all.

EDNA. And it does. It looks very boyish. (*To prompt corner.*)
Doesn't it look boyish, Johnny?

JOHNNY (*off*). Very boyish, Miss Selby.

EDNA. I was only laughing at your suddenly putting in a thing
like that, after our having done this play so many hundreds
of times together and never a little jump in fifteen years until
now – just before a first night.

ARTHUR. All right. All right. Let's forget the whole thing. I'll
say the line standing as still as the Rock of Ages, and looking
just about twice as old – let's go on.

EDNA. It's silly to say that, Arthur. If you feel you're too old
for the part you'll only get a complex about it.

ARTHUR. I am much too old for the part. I'm not seventeen.

EDNA. Well, if it comes to that, darling, I'm not thirteen, but I
shan't let that worry me tonight. It's all up here – (*Taps her
forehead.*) it's not just a question of doing little jumps –

ARTHUR. I am not doing any little jump. That's dead, once and
for all. Now, for God's sake, let's go on.

EDNA. Besides, it's silly to think you don't look young. That
wig is very, very becoming. (*Shields her eyes and looks over
the footlights at the audience.*) Auntie Maud! Are you in
front, dear?

DAME MAUD GOSPORT *appears from the wings. She is
an imposing old lady dressed as the Nurse.*

DAME MAUD. I've just come from in front, dear. What is it?

EDNA. How did you think Arthur looked?

DAME MAUD. Far too old.

EDNA. Oh. Too much light on him?

DAME MAUD. Far too much.

ARTHUR. What about Edna, Auntie Maud? How did she look?

DAME MAUD. Far too old, too.

ARTHUR. Too much light on her too?

DAME MAUD. Yes. Far too much.

EDNA. I don't think Auntie Maud sees very well. Do you, Auntie Maud, dear? (*To* ARTHUR, *in an undertone*.) She's getting so shortsighted, you know, Arthur –

DAME MAUD (*firmly*). Yes, I do. I see very well. I had my specs on, and I was right at the back, and you both looked far too old.

She goes off.

ARTHUR (*calling*). Jack! Jack! Where's the stage manager?

JACK WAKEFIELD, *the stage manager, comes on from the prompt corner. He is a grave-faced young man in the late twenties.*

JACK. Yes, Mr Gosport?

ARTHUR. The lighting for this scene has gone mad. This isn't our plot. There's far too much light. What's gone wrong with it?

JACK. I think the trouble is they've crept in numbers two and three too early. (*Calling up to the flies.*) Will – check your plot, please. Number two and three spots should be down to a quarter instead of full.

VOICE (*from above*). Okay.

JACK. And you've got your floats too high, too. You're burning Mr Gosport up –

EDNA. What about me? I've got an enormous searchlight on me from somewhere out there.

JACK (*looking*). That's the front-of-house, Miss Selby. It's in the plot.

EDNA. Well, take it out –

ARTHUR. No, you can't. You've got to have some light on this scene. We can't have it played as just our two voices coming out of pitch darkness, much as we both might like to.

EDNA. Well, I don't see why you should skulk about in romantic moonlight while I'm on my balcony, being burnt to a cinder by Eddystone Lighthouse.

ARTHUR. Let me see that plot.

DAME MAUD *comes on to join* EDNA *on balcony.*

DAME MAUD. As you've stopped, dear, I thought you wouldn't mind if I gave you one or two teeny little hints about this scene. It's the first time I've seen it from the front. You don't mind an old lady's interference, do you, dear?

EDNA (*rather too sweetly*). No, of course not, Auntie Maud. You know how delighted I always am to have your teeny hints.

JACK *and* ARTHUR *pay no attention to* DAME MAUD, *continuing to rearrange the lighting.*

JACK. Take it right down, Will… That's it.

DAME MAUD (*to* EDNA). Now when I played Juliet I used to rest my hand on my cheek, like this – (*Demonstrates.*) using just the very tips of my fingers. Now as you do it you look just a little like Rodin's *Thinker.*

EDNA. Oh. Do I?

ARTHUR (*lighting*). That's too low. Now bring it up a bit.

JACK. Bring it up, Will.

EDNA. Well, you know, Auntie Maud, dear, tastes have changed a little since you played Juliet with Arthur's father.

DAME MAUD. I know they have, dear, and more's the pity.

EDNA. The theatre's gone through a revolution since 1900.

DAME MAUD. It was 1914 I played Juliet, dear. I remember the date well, because the declaration of war damaged our business so terribly.

EDNA There's been another war since then, Auntie Maud, and I don't think you quite understand the immense change that has come over the theatre in the last few years. You see, dear – I know it's difficult for you to grasp, but the theatre of today has at last acquired a social conscience, and a social purpose. Why else do you think we're opening at this rathole of a theatre instead of the Opera House, Manchester?

DAME MAUD. Oh, I didn't know it was social purpose that brought us here. I thought it was CEMA.

EDNA. CEMA is social purpose.

DAME MAUD. Is it, dear? Fancy!

ARTHUR (*still lighting*). Take it down. That's too high.

JACK (*calling*). Too high, Will.

An old actor, GEORGE CHUDLEIGH, *comes on to the stage. He is dressed as a fifteenth-century Italian peasant, and carries a flute.*

GEORGE (*loudly and with clear articulation*). Faith, we may put up our pipes and begone.

ARTHUR. What?

GEORGE. Oh, am I wrong? I heard my cue, so I came on.

ARTHUR. Well, kindly go off.

GEORGE. Yes. Still, you gave me my cue, you know. You can't say you didn't.

ARTHUR. What is your cue?

GEORGE. Well, it's really a pause, when everyone's stopped speaking.

ARTHUR. My dear Mr –

GEORGE. Chudleigh. George Chudleigh.

ARTHUR. My dear Mr Chudleigh, if every time there's a pause in the play you're going to come on to the stage and speak

that line, it's going to make the plot rather difficult to
follow –

GEORGE. I meant that's just my cue to come on. My real cue is
'High will' –

JACK (*unruffled*). 'Move them no more by crossing their high
will.' He's quite right, Mr Gosport. (*To* GEORGE.) That *is*
your cue, but your line doesn't come till the next act and you
ought to have been paying more attention. Now will you
please get off the stage as we're rather busy.

GEORGE. Well – that's all very well, but you said it, you know.
I heard it quite distinctly. So of course I thought you'd cut a
bit out and so I counted five and on I came.

ARTHUR (*in a fury of impatience*). Get off the stage, you silly
old man –

GEORGE (*stolidly indignant*). Here. Don't you talk to me like
that, young chap. I acted with your father.

ARTHUR. I don't care if you acted with Garrick's father. Get
off the stage!

GEORGE. You'd better be careful, young feller, talking to
people like that. It's not right.

DAME MAUD *now intervenes*. EDNA, *on her balcony, is
sitting down, her back to the commotion, reading a
newspaper.*

DAME MAUD. You say you acted with my brother?

GEORGE. That's right. In this play I was, too. I played Peter.

DAME MAUD. Yes, I remember now. I remember you well.
You were just as incompetent then as you are now.

GEORGE (*under his breath*). That's enough from you, you old
bag!

DAME MAUD (*triumphantly*). There you are! That shows
exactly why you've never got on in the theatre. If you have a
line like that to say, you don't mouth it and throw it away,
you say it right out. It's a glorious word to say –

(*Enunciating*.) bag. Form the word with your lips, like that.
BAG. B-A-G. B – A – G.

ARTHUR. All right, Auntie Maud. All right. (*To* GEORGE.)
Look, my dear chap, just go to the wings – there's a good
fellow – and wait for your scene, which doesn't come for
hours yet, while we get on with our work.

GEORGE. I certainly won't. I've been insulted and I'm leaving.

ARTHUR. Nonsense. You can't leave.

GEORGE. Oh yes, I can. I know my rights. What's more, I'm
not just leaving, I'm retiring. I'm sixty-seven and I'd have
been fifty years on the stage, come April.

DAME MAUD. My dear Mr – er – you really mustn't take on
like this just because –

GEORGE (*brushing her aside*). I've never been a good actor,
and when I look at some that are, I thank God for it. What's
more I've never liked the life – and I've never needed the
money. Why I've gone on all these years mucking about with
never more than a line or two to say, sharing dressing rooms
with chaps I detest, is more than I can fathom. Well, I'm
finished with it all now, anyway. Finished with it for good,
and you don't know how happy that makes me feel.
Goodbye, all.

He goes off. There is a silence after he has gone, broken by
DAME MAUD.

DAME MAUD (*scornfully*). Can't even make an exit properly.

EDNA. Must have a film job.

ARTHUR. Oh. All right. One of the supers can do the pipes
line. Break for an hour for tea, but don't strike this set. I
want to rehearse the farewell scene before the show.

JACK. Yes, Mr Gosport. (*Calling*.) Break for an hour for tea,
everyone! Back at 5.30, please! Curtain up at 7.30.

ARTHUR. Then I'll rehearse the duel.

JACK. Yes, Mr Gosport.

ARTHUR. And I could see those girls for *The Winter's Tale*.

JACK. Yes, Mr Gosport.

ARTHUR. And then, if there's time, I can rehearse the jig.

JACK. Yes, Mr Gosport. (*Goes towards wings*.)

DAME MAUD. Oh, Jack – send someone out for some sandwiches for me – and a bottle of Guinness, would you?

JACK. Yes, Dame Maud.

DAME MAUD. Better make it a couple of bottles. It's so good for my back.

JACK. Yes, Dame Maud.

JACK goes off.

DAME MAUD. Goodbye, my children. I'm sure from what I've seen it's all going to be splendid.

She exits.

JOHNNY comes on with sandwiches for ARTHUR, *and then goes out.*

ARTHUR. Sandwich, dear?

EDNA (*to* ARTHUR). No thank you, darling. I'll have a proper tea for us in our room, my darling.

ARTHUR. Thank you, darling.

EDNA. Don't worry, my precious. That wig is a dream. And you can do your little jump if you want to.

ARTHUR. No, thank you, darling. Edna – I'm not too old for the part, am I?

EDNA. No; of course not, my angel. Or, if you are, then I am.

ARTHUR. But you're three years younger, aren't you?

EDNA. What's three among so many?

She goes out through her bedroom window.

Enter JOHNNY.

Two young men, dressed as HALBERDIERS *and trailing spears, cross the stage at back, chatting to each other in confidential whispers.*

ARTHUR. Johnny, draw the tabs and rehearse some of the lighting cues during the break, will you. (*Over the footlights.*) Miss Fishlock? Would you come to my room for a moment? I want you to take some notes on *The Winter's Tale*. (*Turns and sees the young men.*) Would you come here, you two?

They both obey with alacrity.

(*To one of them.*) Just say – Faith, we may put up our pipes and begone.

FIRST HALBERDIER (*in a flat, faintly Cockney accent*). Faith, we may put up our pipes and begone.

ARTHUR (*to the other*). Now you.

SECOND HALBERDIER (*going much too far, vocally and in gesture*). Faith, we may put up our pipes and begone.

ARTHUR (*pointing to* FIRST HALBERDIER). Right. You'll do it.

FIRST HALBERDIER (*transported*). You mean – I'm going to have a line to say, Mr Gosport?

ARTHUR. Yes. (*Hands him the script.*) I'll rehearse you in a few minutes.

MISS FISHLOCK *comes on.*

Ah, Miss Fishlock. Would you get in touch with the London Office at once and inform Mr Wilmot that the six girls he sent up specially for *The Winter's Tale* are quite out of the question.

MISS FISHLOCK. Yes, Mr Gosport.

FIRST HALBERDIER. Oh, Mr Gosport! (*To* SECOND HALBERDIER.) Oh bad luck, Cyril.

Exit MISS FISHLOCK *and* ARTHUR.

SECOND HALBERDIER (*they drift away, peering at the script together*). I bet it was because you picked up his gloves at the station on Friday.

He disappears.

FIRST HALBERDIER *looks round the stage cautiously, and, finding himself alone, goes down to the footlights.*

FIRST HALBERDIER (*in a hoarse whisper, across the footlights*). Mum! Mum!

JACK *appears, unseen by the* FIRST HALBERDIER.

I've got a part. It's only a line, but it's awfully important... Yes, isn't it wonderful?

JACK (*approaching him*). Who are you talking to?

FIRST HALBERDIER (*confused*). Oh, Mr Wakefield. I didn't see you. It's only my mother. She's up there. (*Waves towards the upper circle.*)

JACK. Then I'm afraid you must ask her to go. You know the rule about strangers in front at rehearsal.

FIRST HALBERDIER. Oh, but can't she stay and hear me speak my line?

JACK. No, I'm afraid not. She'll have to come back at 7.30 when we start.

FIRST HALBERDIER. But she has to get back to Birmingham tonight. She only came for the day –

JACK (*firmly*). I'm extremely sorry, but rules are rules and Mr and Mrs Gosport are very strict about this particular one. She shouldn't be here at all.

He turns away as a man in the costume of Tybalt (FREDERICK INGRAM) *comes on to the stage with a cup of tea and a sausage roll.*

INGRAM (*to* JACK). What the hell does he want me for?

JACK. The duel.

INGRAM. Oh, my God! Not again!

The FIRST HALBERDIER *has meanwhile been gesticulating across the footlights to his mother, making uncomplimentary and furtive gestures towards* JACK. *When he has conveyed his meaning he goes off.*

I'm slipping across to The Feathers for a quick one. Do you think I've got time?

JACK. Yes, Mr Ingram. I'll warn you.

INGRAM *goes off. The assistant stage manager* (JOHNNY) *puts his head on.*

JOHNNY. 'Ere – there's a baby in a pram in the wings. Is that a prop in the play?

JACK. Not unless they've considerably rewritten it. Is it alive?

JOHNNY. Oh, I don't know. I'll just see.

His head momentarily disappears. We hear, faintly, a baby's gurgle. JOHNNY*'s head reappears.*

Yes. It's alive. What shall I do with it?

JACK. I suppose you'd better leave it there. Presumably it belongs to someone. My God! What with mums in front and babies in the wings it's not so much a dress rehearsal as old home week.

A nondescript, rather shabbily dressed girl of about twenty (MURIEL), *accompanied by a soldier* (TOM), *about ten years older, have come timidly on to the stage and are staring about them.* JOHNNY*'s head has meanwhile disappeared.*

Yes? What do you want?

MURIEL (*in a strong Midland accent*). Could I speak to my dad, please?

JACK. And who may your dad be?

MURIEL. He's an actor.

JACK. Then I'm afraid you've come to the wrong theatre. Try The Palace of Varieties across the street.

MR BURTON, *the theatre manager, has come on.*

BURTON. Good evening, Mr Wakefield.

JACK. Good evening, Mr Burton.

BURTON. I hope you find our theatre to your satisfaction.

JACK. How are our bookings?

BURTON. Not bad. Not half bad, considering what the show is. Of course, we've never had these two up here before, you know, but it's a big help that feller Fred Ingram being in that picture at the Super.

MURIEL (*to* JACK). Look – I'm sure it *is* this theatre –

JACK. No, my dear. They've got a sort of circus here this week. The Palace is what you want. Through that door there, up the stairs and into the street.

He moves away again. MURIEL *and* TOM *go off slowly.*

BURTON. Funny for them to choose to open up here, I must say –

JACK. Social purpose, Mr Burton.

BURTON. Social purpose? Now what the blazes is that when it's at home?

JACK. As far as I can see it means playing Shakespeare to audiences who'd rather go to the films; while audiences who'd rather go to Shakespeare are driven to the films because they haven't got Shakespeare to go to. It's all got something to do with the new Britain and apparently it's an absolutely splendid idea.

ARTHUR *comes on, now in a dressing gown.*

Here's Mr Gosport. He can tell you all about it. This is Mr Burton, sir. The theatre manager.

ARTHUR. Oh, how do you do? My wife and I are simply thrilled to be opening in your beautiful theatre and this delightful town.

BURTON. Thank you, Mr Gosport, and I can assure you it's a great honour for us all to have you both up here.

ARTHUR. Thank you. As a matter of fact you've always been very kind to us here in Sheffield –

BURTON. But it's next week you're playing Sheffield, Mr Gosport.

ARTHUR. Oh! What's this town, then?

BURTON. Brackley.

ARTHUR. Oh yes, of course. They added a week, didn't they? How idiotic of them!

BURTON. That's all right, Mr Gosport. Great men are always a bit absent-minded.

ARTHUR. Brackley. Of course it is. (*With a sudden change of expression.*) Brackley! Good Lord!

JACK. What's the matter?

ARTHUR. I was just remembering something. Brackley! Good heavens!

JACK. Is anything wrong, Mr Gosport?

ARTHUR *is lost in a reverie.* BURTON *looks at* JACK, *a trifle bewildered.* JACK *touches his forehead.* BURTON *nods.*

ARTHUR. Tell me, Mr – er – hrrhm – , is there a square place in your town with a perfectly repulsive building in glazed brick with a ridiculous dome on top?

BURTON (*doubtfully*). The Civic Centre?

ARTHUR (*impatiently*). Yes, yes. And then, dead opposite, is there an enormous white concrete-and-glass object that looks just like a public lavatory?

BURTON (*too hurt even to protest*). The Civic Library, Mr Gosport.

JACK (*hastily*). Do you know this town, then, Mr Gosport?

ARTHUR. Yes. Only too well.

JACK *manages to get in a nudge.*

Only too well. I was here as a boy in repertory.

BURTON. When exactly were you here, Mr Gosport? (*Getting out notebook and pencil.*) Could you pin it to a definite date? I ought to ring up the *Argus* about this.

ARTHUR. Well, let me see now. (*Ponders deeply.*) Yes, I can tell you exactly. It was the year Gladys Cooper opened in *The Sign of the Door.*

BURTON. I'm afraid I don't remember that, Mr Gosport. (*To* JACK.) Do you?

JACK. No. (*To* ARTHUR.) I suppose you couldn't remember anything else that happened that year? A war, or something like that?

ARTHUR. No, I don't think there was a war. Wait a moment – I do remember something that happened that year. There was some sort of commotion –

JACK. A commotion? An earthquake?

ARTHUR. No, no. Something to do with trains. They didn't run. And newspapers too. There weren't any notices. And then I was made to drive a tram, for some reason –

JACK. 1926. The general strike.

ARTHUR. Thank you. That's right. That's what it was called. The general strike.

BURTON (*writing down the date*). 1926.

ARTHUR. Excuse me… I must get a cup of tea before I look at six girls…

He goes off.

BURTON. Bit scatterbrained, isn't he?

JACK. I doubt if you can scatter a void.

BURTON. I thought he was supposed to be an intellectual sort of chap.

JACK. He's an actor, Mr Burton.

BURTON. Now perhaps you wouldn't mind giving me a bit more dope on the Gosports for the *Argus*.

JACK. All right, but very quickly. I've got a hundred things to do.

BURTON. How long have they been married?

JACK. Fifteen years.

BURTON. Any children?

JACK. One – little Basil –

BURTON. Oh. And how old is little Basil?

JACK. Thirteen.

BURTON. Up here?

JACK. No. At school –

BURTON. Going to be an actor too?

JACK. Judging by his behaviour, yes. Besides – he's a Gosport.

BURTON. I see. Now how would you describe these Gosports? Would we offend anyone if we called them the most famous married couple in the theatre?

JACK. You wouldn't offend the Gosports, Mr Burton, which is the main thing. Besides it's reasonably true.

BURTON. Always act together, don't they?

JACK. Yes.

BURTON. Always as husband and wife?

JACK. No. Usually as lover and mistress. The audience prefers that – it gives them such a cosy feeling to know they're really married after all.

BURTON. Now, about this tour. How long is it?

JACK. Sixteen weeks out, then London –

BURTON. Oh. They *are* going to London, then?

JACK. Only for four weeks. If you play in the West End for longer than that you become commercial.

BURTON. I see. What after that?

JACK. Belgrade, Bucharest, Warsaw, Riga, and Moscow.

BURTON. Oh. What about the Iron Curtain?

JACK. The Gosports could make any curtain rise.

BURTON. What plays are they taking?

ARTHUR, *tea in hand, wanders on and begins fussing mildly in the background, removing a pot of artificial flowers from one place on the stage and putting it in another; then changing his mind and putting it back again.*

JACK. *Romeo*, *The Winter's Tale*, *Macbeth*, and a modern play in verse called *Follow the Leviathan to My Father's Grave*.

BURTON. What's that about?

JACK. Here's Mr Gosport, he'll tell you.

BURTON. What's the new play about, Mr Gosport?

ARTHUR. Death. My wife's got the best part in it. I only play the pencil-sharpener in the last act.

He replaces the pot once more and wanders off.

BURTON Well, perhaps he'll tell more about it to the *Argus* critic.

JACK. I doubt it.

ARTHUR *reappears*.

ARTHUR. There's a baby here, in the wings. It looks exactly like someone I know. Who is it?

JACK. I've no idea, I'm afraid.

ARTHUR. It's very careless of people, leaving babies in the wings. There might be a very nasty accident. Somebody might easily trip over it and ruin their exit. See that it's removed before rehearsal.

JACK. Yes, Mr Gosport.

ARTHUR. And in future, if people bring babies to the theatre, see that they're kept in the proper place.

JACK. Yes, Mr Gosport. Where's that?

ARTHUR. I don't know.

He goes off again.

JACK. Well, is there any more help I can give you, Mr Burton?

BURTON. No, thanks. I think that's all. It only remains for me to wish you a very successful opening, which I'm sure you'll have.

JACK. Thank you very much.

They shake hands. MURIEL *and* TOM *appear suddenly on Juliet's balcony.*

MURIEL (*attacked with vertigo*). Oo – Tom! Look where we've got ourselves to!

JACK. Madam – will you and your friend kindly leave this theatre?

MURIEL. No, I won't. I've told you. I want to see my dad.

JACK. And I've told you your dad isn't here.

MURIEL. Oh, yes, he is. He's not at The Palace, like you said. He's here. I've seen his name on the posters.

JACK. Well, you can't see him now, anyway. Anyway, who is your dad?

MURIEL. Gosport's the name.

JACK. Gosport?

MURIEL. Yes. Arthur Gosport. He's an actor.

JACK. Oh. I see.

He signs urgently to the prompt corner. JOHNNY *appears.*

So you're the daughter of Arthur Gosport, are you?

MURIEL. Yes, that's right. And this is my husband.

TOM. How do?

JACK. I'm most delighted to meet you both. I simply can't apologise enough for having been so very rude. (*To* JOHNNY.) Oh, Johnny. This lady is Mr Gosport's daughter, and this is her husband. Would you be so kind as to – er – look after them both? Just – er – show them around, would you?

He makes a quick, violent gesture of his thumb, unseen by the two on the balcony. JOHNNY *nods.*

JOHNNY. Okay, Mr Wakefield.

He goes off.

JACK. Now, Miss Gosport –

MURIEL (*giggling*). Mrs Palmer.

JACK. I do beg your pardon, Mrs Palmer. Now, if you and your husband would be so very kind as to step through that window there and down the steps, you'll find such a nice gentleman who's going to take such very good care of you both.

MURIEL. Oh. Thanks – you're a pal. Come on, Tom.

She disappears from view. TOM *waves cheerfully to* JACK *and follows her.*

BURTON. Lor' love us! What will they think up next?

JACK. Amazing, isn't it?

BURTON (*shaking his head, sadly*). It's a funny world ours, isn't it?

JACK. Side-splitting.

The FIRST HALBERDIER *comes on mouthing and muttering anxiously to himself.*

BURTON *exits.*

JACK *shakes his head wearily. Then looks at his watch.* JOHNNY *reappears.*

All right?

JOHNNY. I'll lock 'em in one of the downstairs rooms. I'd better not shove 'em out as the doorman's off and they might get in again.

JACK. Quite right. Which room will you put them in?

JOHNNY. I'll put them in number three. There are six other girls there waiting for someone.

JACK (*wearily*). I wonder whose daughters they are. Okay, Johnny. Thanks.

He goes off as the FIRST HALBERDIER *approaches* JACK.

FIRST HALBERDIER. Mr Wakefield, do you think it ought to be: Faith, we may put up our PIPES and begone, or FAITH, we may put UP our pipes and begone?

JACK What about, Faith, we may put up our pipes and – (*Roaring.*) BEGONE?

FIRST HALBERDIER. That doesn't sound quite right to me.

JACK. It sounds awfully right to me. What's happened to your mum?

FIRST HALBERDIER. Oh, she's gone.

JACK (*grimly*). That's very lucky for *her*.

A very good-looking, smartly dressed girl (JOYCE LANGLAND) *appears on the stage and stands, evidently a little awed by her surroundings.*

The FIRST HALBERDIER *wanders off, still muttering.*

JOYCE. Jack –

JACK (*surprised*). Joyce! (*Approaches her and kisses her warmly.*) Why on earth didn't you let me know you were coming up?

JOYCE. I didn't have time.

JACK. What do you mean, you didn't have time?

JOYCE. I've got some news for you which I had to tell you myself, so I just jumped on the first train.

JACK. Oh, darling! How wonderful!

JOYCE (*disappointed*). You've guessed.

JACK. Your father's changed his mind. Darling, you're a magician. How did you work it?

JOYCE. You worked it. He was terribly impressed with your letter.

JACK. So he should be.

JOYCE. Then I told him your war record.

JACK. That was a mistake, wasn't it?

JOYCE. You got the DFC.

JACK. Only because the CO liked the pantomime I produced for the chaps. I say, darling, are we rich?

JOYCE. We'll pay super-tax, anyway.

JACK. Oh, darling, how marvellous! I don't have to work any more?

JOYCE. Not in the theatre, anyway.

JACK. Oh. But I do have to work?

JOYCE. He's going to take you into the firm.

JACK. Oh. I thought there was a catch.

JOYCE. Darling, it's not a catch. Jack – it's not that you don't want to give up the theatre, is it?

JACK. Good Lord, no! I'd give up the theatre tomorrow if I could.

JOYCE. Well, now you can.

There is a pause, broken by the FIRST HALBERDIER, *who has wandered on to the stage a few seconds before.*

FIRST HALBERDIER. Faith, we may put up OUR pipes and begone.

JACK. Look, old chap – do you mind awfully going and doing that somewhere else? I've got things on my mind.

FIRST HALBERDIER. Sorry, Mr Wakefield. This is my great chance, you know – and I don't want to muck it up. (*Muttering.*) That's it. I know. Faith, we may put up OUR pipes and begone.

He goes off.

JACK. Darling, I think I'd better finish the tour.

JOYCE (*horrified*). The whole tour – forty-six weeks?

JACK. No, no. Only England. After London they'll have to get someone else. But I can't let them down without fair warning.

JOYCE. No. I see that. There's only one thing I'm frightened of though, Jack. Shall I tell you what it is?

JACK. That I haven't the guts to leave them at all?

JOYCE. It's not only the Gosports I'm worrying about. It's the theatre.

JACK. The Gosports are the theatre. There is no theatre apart from the Gosports.

JOYCE. Darling, don't exaggerate.

JACK. I'm not. I mean the Gosports are eternal. They're the theatre at its worst and its best. They're true theatre, because they're entirely self-centred, entirely exhibitionist, and entirely dotty, and because they make no compromise whatever with the outside world.

JOYCE. Then what about this idea of theirs of theatre with a social purpose?

JACK. Theatre with a social purpose, indeed! It's a contradiction in terms. Good citizenship and good theatre don't go together. They never have and they never will. All through the ages, from Burbage downwards, the theatre – the true theatre – has consisted of blind, antisocial, self-sufficient, certifiable Gosports. The point is that if I have the courage to leave the Gosports, I have the courage to leave the theatre.

JOYCE. And have you?

JACK. Yes. I hate the theatre. I shall leave the theatre without the faintest regret, and for a week afterwards I shall barely draw a sober breath in celebration.

JOYCE (*with a sigh of relief*). And I'll be at your side in that. Good. Will you go and tell them now, then?

JACK. Now?

JOYCE. Yes. There's a break on, isn't there?

JACK (*slowly*). Yes. Is this a test of my courage?

JOYCE. That's it.

JACK. All right. I might as well get it over with. Besides, I'm
giving them plenty of notice, aren't I?

JOYCE (*smiling*). Yes. Plenty.

JACK (*annoyed*). I'm not in the least afraid of them, you know,
if that's what you think.

EDNA, *in dressing gown and chewing a sandwich, wanders
on from the wings.*

EDNA. I'm a bit worried about the balcony, Jack. It seems very
wobbly to me.

JACK. It's being seen to, Miss Selby. Er – Miss Selby –

EDNA (*turning*). Yes?

JACK. Could I introduce Miss Langland?

EDNA. Oh yes. How do you do? (*Shakes hands.*) You're a
serving wench, aren't you?

JACK. Er – no. She's not in the company at all. As a matter of
fact, Miss Selby – she's the girl I'm going to marry.

EDNA. Marry! My dear, how wonderful! How simply
wonderful! Oh, Jack, darling, I'm so glad. (*Embraces him
warmly. To* JOYCE.) And you too, my dear. (*Kisses her.*) So
pretty you are, and so young and what an enchanting little
frock! Oh, I'm so happy for you both, I feel I want to cry and
ruin my make-up. Arthur must be your best man, and I'll be
godmother to your first. When's the wedding to be?

JACK (*exchanging glances with* JOYCE). After the provincial
tour – when we come to London.

EDNA. Oh, good! (*To* JOYCE.) It would have been far too long
a time to wait for him, wouldn't it – forty-six weeks?

JOYCE (*surprised*). Yes. I did feel that, I'm afraid.

EDNA. Don't be afraid, dear. You're quite right to be impatient.
I was, when I married Arthur. (*Strokes* JOYCE's *face.*) Dear

little child. I'm so happy for you. So you'll be coming to Europe with us, will you?

JOYCE. Er – no, Miss Selby. I won't.

EDNA. No? Well, perhaps you're wise. It's going to be rather uncomfortable for all of us, I expect. Still, won't you miss him, being gone all that time?

JACK. Well – the fact is, Miss Selby – you see – I – er – well – this is the point – I'm not sure that I'm going to Europe myself.

EDNA. Not going to Europe? (*Looks mildly surprised then appears to see daylight.*) Oh, I know what you mean. Some nasty creature must have sneaked to you about what Arthur was saying the other day about Ronnie Williams coming to stage-manage for us. But you mustn't worry, my darling. It was only because Ronnie Williams stage-managed for us for so long – practically before you were born, my darling – and Arthur heard he was out of a job, and you know how tactless he is, the poor old thing – but he really didn't mean it, I know he didn't –

JACK (*desperately*). Look, Miss Selby – it's got nothing to do with Ronnie Williams –

EDNA. You're hurt, my precious. I'm so sorry. But I can promise you most faithfully that there was never, never any question of our not taking you to Europe. We all love you and admire you far too much –

JACK. Thank you very much, Miss Selby, but –

EDNA. Now I don't want to hear anything more about it. Just forget the whole thing and pretend it never happened. You're coming with us to Europe. I promise you. Goodbye, you dear things. (*Blows them a fond kiss.*) You look so pretty, the two of you, standing there together.

She goes off.

JACK (*to* JOYCE). Look, darling, perhaps a dress rehearsal isn't the best moment to break it to them. What about tomorrow – or after the first night?

JOYCE. Or after Sheffield, or after London, or after the European tour? No, Jack, darling, something tells me that if you don't do it now, during this break, you never will –

JACK. I could write them a letter –

JOYCE. I thought you said you weren't afraid of them?

ARTHUR *wanders on and makes straight for the flower pot, removing it, in the background, to another spot.*

JACK. I know. I'll tell *him*. He's really much easier to deal with than she is.

JOYCE (*indicating* ARTHUR). Well, now's your chance, then.

JACK *starts violently; then braces himself and takes* JOYCE *by the hand up to* ARTHUR.

JACK. Oh, Mr Gosport.

ARTHUR. Yes.

JACK. Could I introduce Miss Langland?

ARTHUR. Oh. How do you do. Have you read *The Winter's Tale*?

JOYCE. Er – no. I'm afraid I haven't.

ARTHUR. Well, it's not a difficult part. It's about a girl who's abandoned by her father when she's a baby, and then many years later they meet –

JACK. Er – Miss Langland isn't here about *The Winter's Tale*, Mr Gosport. (*In a firm, measured voice.*) She's my fiancée, we're getting married after the provincial tour, and I'm not coming with you to Europe.

ARTHUR. Yes. I see, my dear fellow. Now what about those girls for *Winter's Tale*? Are they here?

JACK. Yes, I think so. Did you hear what I said, Mr Gosport?

ARTHUR. Yes, of course. I think I'd better see those girls straight away. Have them in, one by one, would you? (*Puts the pot in another place.*)

JACK. Yes, Mr Gosport. (*Calling.*) Johnny. Are the girls here for *Winter's Tale*?

JOHNNY (*off*). Yes. Seven of them.

JACK. That's right. Mr Gosport will see them now, separately.

JOHNNY (*off*). Okay.

ARTHUR (*indicating pot*). How do you like it here, Jack?

JACK. Much better.

ARTHUR (*to* JOYCE). What do you think, Miss – er – Hrrhm?

JOYCE. I think it's charming, there.

ARTHUR. No. I don't think I like it there very much. (*Removes it.*)

JACK. Mr Gosport, I don't think you quite grasped what I said just now.

ARTHUR (*annoyed at the implication*). Of course I did, my dear fellow. You said you thought the pot looked better there, but I don't agree –

JACK. No. Before that. I told you I was getting married –

ARTHUR. Getting married? I'm absolutely delighted, my dear chap. (*Shakes hands.*) Who to?

EDNA *comes on.*

ARTHUR. Edna, I've thought of an entirely new way of dying.

EDNA. Have you darling? How exciting.

ARTHUR. Bring on the tomb, someone.

JACK. Yes, Mr Gosport. (*Calling.*) Johnny, give me a hand with the tomb.

JOHNNY (*coming on*). Yes, Mr Wakefield.

He and JACK *bring forward the tomb and* JOHNNY *goes off.*

ARTHUR (*going over to* JOYCE). Now, young lady, perhaps you would be kind enough to take up a position there – thank you. (*To* EDNA.) The beauty of it is in its simplicity. Now I must get you something to lie on.

He takes a mackintosh from JOYCE *and spreads it over the tomb.* EDNA *lies on it.*

Thank you.

JACK. Look, Mr Gosport, there's something I've got to tell you before you die.

ARTHUR. Well, if she can't do the quick-change in time, she'll just have to wear the black velvet all through.

JACK. But Mr Gos–

ARTHUR That's all there is to it. I don't want to hear another word about it. (*Adopting his dying pose.*)

Now. Come, bitter conduct, come, unsavoury guide!
Thou desperate pilot, now at once run on,
The dashing rocks thy sea-sick weary bark!
Here's to my love! (*Drinks.*) – Oh true apothecary!
Thy drugs are quick. – Thus with a kiss I die.

And a very spectacular death it is. JOYCE, *despite her prejudice, is thrilled.*

JOYCE (*to* JACK). That was wonderful!

ARTHUR (*overhearing*). Oh, did you like it, Miss – Hrrhm? I'm so glad. You didn't think it was too much?

JOYCE. Oh no. Not a bit – I thought it was thrilling.

EDNA (*sitting up*). Jack, darling, don't you think your little friend must be feeling awfully cold, standing on this draughty stage in that thin little frock? Wouldn't she be much better off in a nice warm dressing room?

JACK (*resignedly*). Yes, Miss Selby. (*To* JOYCE.) Darling, run along to my room, would you? It's number fourteen on the second floor. I'll join you when I can.

JOYCE. All right. (*As she goes.*) Now, don't let me down, Jack. Before the break is up.

EDNA. Such a sweet little face.

JACK. Before the break is up. I promise.

JOYCE *goes out.*

EDNA. Arthur, it's a lovely death, but I'm not absolutely sure it doesn't go on perhaps a hair too long. I don't think we'll put it in tonight.

ARTHUR (*knowing he has lost*). All right, darling. I just thought it was worth trying – that was all.

The FIRST HALBERDIER *comes on, still muttering*.

FIRST HALBERDIER. Oh, Mr Gosport. Are you ready for me yet?

ARTHUR. No. In a minute. I'm seeing some girls first. Just wait there.

He motions him to a corner of the stage, where the FIRST HALBERDIER *sits, mouthing intermittently*.

All right, Jack. Ready for *The Winter's Tale*.

JACK (*calling*). All right, Johnny. Send the first lady on, will you?

JOHNNY (*off*). Okay.

JACK (*calling*). What is the lady's name, please?

Whispers off.

JOHNNY (*off*). Muriel Palmer.

JACK (*writing it down*). Muriel Palmer.

And MURIEL PALMER *comes on, followed at a few yards' interval by* TOM. JACK, *busy with his notebook, does not immediately look up*.

MURIEL (*with a joyous cry, pointing at* ARTHUR). There he is! That's my dad! Daddy, I'm your daughter, and you're my dad.

ARTHUR. Er – what text are you using, Miss, er – hrrhm?

JACK (*interposing quickly*). Excuse me, Mr Gosport, but I know about this young lady. She's been annoying us all the evening. (*To* MURIEL.) How did you get out of that room?

MURIEL. A young man came and unlocked us and told me and six other girls to come on the stage separately as Mr Gosport was waiting for us –

JACK. Oh God! All right. Well, now, are you going to go quietly or shall I have to ring up for the police?

MURIEL. Ring up the police? Go ahead. I don't mind. I haven't done anything wrong. I just want a few words with my dad, that's all. That's my dad, all right. I recognise him from Mum's picture on the piano.

TOM. Even in this country you can't arrest a girl for talking to her dad, you know.

MURIEL. You can't scare me, young man.

JACK. All right. (*Calling.*) Johnny! Ring up the police station and ask them to send a man round. We're having trouble.

ARTHUR (*to* JACK). Do I understand that this lady claims that I'm her father?

MURIEL. Your name is Gosport, isn't it?

ARTHUR. Arthur Gosport. Yes.

MURIEL (*chattily*). Well, I'm your daughter, Muriel. You've never seen me, because I was born after you left Mum. This is my husband, Tom – he's your son-in-law.

TOM. How do?

MURIEL. And I've brought someone else along that I thought you'd like to meet. Tom! (*Signs to him to go to the wings.*)

TOM. Okay, Mu.

ARTHUR. Just a minute. (*To* MURIEL.) You mentioned just now a character called Mum. Could you be more explicit, please? Where does this Mum person live?

MURIEL. Same old place. Number twenty-one Upper Brecon Road.

ARTHUR. Opposite a puce, rectangular building – with a notice board outside, saying Thy Days are Numbered?

MURIEL. That's right. The Baptist Chapel.

ARTHUR. And is Mum's name – Florence?

MURIEL. Flossie. That's right.

ARTHUR (*whimpering*). Flossie! (*With a wail.*) Oh, no, no. It can't be!

MURIEL. Oh yes, it is, Dad.

EDNA. Arthur! You can't mean –

ARTHUR. Yes, yes, oh yes! It's true. I know it now. (*Pointing tragically.*) You've only to look at her face to see it. The living image of her dreadful mother.

MURIEL. Well, really! That's a nice way to talk, I must say –

JACK (*taking charge*). Look, Mr Gosport – as we've never seen the lady's dreadful mother, perhaps there's some other way we could test her story. (*To* MURIEL.) When were you born?

MURIEL. January 15th, 1927.

JACK (*to* ARTHUR). When did you last see Flossie?

ARTHUR. Don't cross-examine me! I don't know. I can only tell you that I am absolutely convinced of the truth of this girl's statement. This is my daughter, Mabel –

MURIEL. Muriel. Mu for short.

ARTHUR. My daughter, Muriel. Mu for short.

He sinks down on to a stool, his head in his hands. EDNA *loyally goes to his side to comfort him.*

(*To* MURIEL.) Why are you here? What do you want?

MURIEL. Want? I don't want anything. Just to say hullo, that's all. It seemed silly being in the same town, and for us not even to meet each other. Mum didn't want me to come, but I thought Dad'll be interested to see what I look like, and to meet his son-in-law. Besides I've got such a nice little surprise for you. (*Calling.*) Come on, Tom. I want to introduce you to your grandson.

TOM *appears, wheeling a pram tenderly towards the group, who are too frozen with horror to move.*

ARTHUR (*at length*). My – grandson?

MURIEL. That's right, Dad. Come and look.

Very slowly ARTHUR *rises and, with* EDNA *on one side and* JACK *on* the other, gazes down on the pram. MURIEL *and* TOM *complete the group. There is a long pause.*

ARTHUR (*slowly, at length*). It looks – (*With a sob.*) like Beerbohm Tree –

EDNA (*hopelessly*). No, darling. The terrible thing is – it looks awfully like you.

ARTHUR. Don't say that, Edna!

MURIEL. Yes, he's the image of his grandpa, isn't he? The ickle, chicka-widdy-biddy woo. Go on, Grandpa, tickle his little tummy.

ARTHUR. I refuse to tickle his little tummy.

EDNA (*to* TOM). How old is it?

TOM. Five months. You're Edna Selby, aren't you?

EDNA. Yes.

TOM. I saw you in Shakespeare once, in Birmingham. You were the Queen, weren't you, when Mr Gosport was Hamlet?

EDNA. I have played it – yes.

TOM (*cheerfully*). Well then in a sort of way, that makes you our little Ted's great-grandmama, doesn't it?

EDNA. No, it doesn't. Not in any sort of way, and please, don't say it does. (*Reproachfully.*) Arthur – how could you!

ARTHUR (*pointing to the pram*). I am not responsible for Ted.

EDNA (*pointing to* MURIEL). But you are responsible for Mu.

ARTHUR (*tragically*). I was a mere boy – a wild, hotheaded, irresponsible, passionate boy – a Romeo of seventeen –

EDNA. And your Juliet was Flossie.

ARTHUR. She was my landlady's daughter. I loved her, for a time, with all my heart and mind. She loved me too, in her way – but not enough. She never even came to the theatre to see me act. Of course it had to end, as all such mad, youthful follies must.

EDNA (*pointing to the pram*). It didn't have to end in this.

ARTHUR. And I say unto you, the sins of the fathers shall be visited upon the children even unto the third and fourth generation. You know the line –

EDNA. It seems to have got up to the fourth generation far too quick. (*Pointing to the pram.*) Oh, Arthur, it's not in my nature to reproach you for what is past and done, but I do think you've been terribly, terribly foolhardy. (*To* TOM.) Please remove this.

TOM. Okay. If that's the way you feel –

MURIEL (*to baby*). Didn't they appreciate him, then? Come along, then, my ickywicky-chick-a-boo! (*Begins to wheel the pram out.*) Come along, then! Say ta-ta for now, Granddaddy –

ARTHUR (*sinking again into an attitude of tragic despair*). Oh, my God! Edna! What am I to do?

Once more EDNA *takes his hand in silent but loyal sympathy.*

The PALMERS *wheel their baby out.*

There is a pause, broken by the FIRST HALBERDIER, *who, throughout the preceding scene, has been mouthing intermittently in the background, more or less oblivious of what has been going on.*

FIRST HALBERDIER (*attempting a new reading*). Faith, we may put UP our PIPES and begone.

ARTHUR. Jack, what am I to do?

JACK (*reassuringly*). Well, Mr Gosport, they haven't bothered you at all for twenty years. I don't see any reason why they should in the future.

ARTHUR. Yes – but that child! (*With a shudder.*) That horrifying child!

JACK. No one need know about that. Ask your dau– Mrs Palmer, to keep the whole thing secret; and if I might venture to suggest it, send an occasional little present to them for the baby.

EDNA. A nice little box of jujubes, flavoured with prussic acid.

ARTHUR. I don't think it's in quite the best of taste to make a joke of that sort, Edna. After all, the creature is my grandson. (*In agony again*.) Oh, God! My grandson!

EDNA. Never mind, my darling. These things can happen to any of us.

ARTHUR. But why, when I'm playing Romeo of all parts? Why couldn't it have turned up when I was playing Lear?

EDNA. That's life, my darling.

ARTHUR. Of course we shall have to cancel the performance now.

JACK. Look, Mr Gosport – I really don't think you'll find it necessary to do that –

ARTHUR. How can I play a boy of seventeen with a grandson in the wings, mocking me with that repulsive leer of his, every time I go on?

JACK. Because it won't be in the wings. First thing tomorrow morning I shall go and see – er – Mrs Palmer's mother. I'd better have her address again.

ARTHUR. Twenty-one Upper Brecon Road.

JACK (*writing it down*). Thank you. And what is her name?

EDNA. Flossie.

JACK. I know. I meant her surname.

ARTHUR. Gosport, I suppose.

JACK. Gosport?

EDNA. What an odd coincidence!

JACK. Mr Gosport – did you – did you marry Flossie?

ARTHUR. Oh yes. She made rather a point of it, I remember.

EDNA. Arthur! You mean your daughter isn't illegitimate?

ARTHUR. Oh no. She's perfectly legitimate, I think.

EDNA (*annoyed*). Well, really? Of course that puts an entirely different complexion on the whole thing. It's going to make *me* look very silly – if that gets out.

ARTHUR. It all happened such a long time ago, darling, and I really didn't see why I should bother you with the whole, rather sordid, story.

JACK (*quietly*). Mr Gosport – when did you divorce your first wife?

ARTHUR Let me see, now. I left her to take a part in a revival of *The Passing of the Third Floor Back* at Barnes.

JACK. I said, when did you divorce her? This is rather important. You did divorce her, didn't you?

ARTHUR. Yes, of course I did, my dear fellow. I remember perfectly.

JACK. Did you divorce her or did she divorce you?

ARTHUR. We divorced each other, my dear chap.

JACK. In law that isn't quite possible, Mr Gosport. Who was awarded the decree nisi – you or your wife?

ARTHUR. Decree nisi? What's that?

JACK. It's the decision awarded by the judge in a divorce action.

ARTHUR. A judge? I don't remember a judge. I'm sure if there'd been a judge, I'd have remembered. There was a solicitor – I know that – and a lot of documents to sign –

JACK (*voice becoming gradually edged with horror as the truth becomes clearer*). Mr Gosport – one solicitor and a lot of documents don't make a divorce, you know.

ARTHUR. My dear fellow, don't fuss! Everything was perfectly legal and in order, I assure you.

JACK. You don't think it might just have been a deed of separation that you signed, and not a divorce at all?

ARTHUR. Of course it was a divorce. It must have been a divorce. The solicitor's name was Jenkins. He had Commissioner of Oaths on his glass door, I remember.

MURIEL *and* TOM *wander on.*

MURIEL. Hullo, Dad. Just been having a look round the stage. Don't mind, do you?

JACK (*urgently*). Mrs Palmer, if I ask you a straight question, will you please give me a straight answer?

MURIEL. All right. Fire away.

JACK. Is your mother divorced?

MURIEL. Divorced? Mum? Of course not.

JACK (*quietly*). Thank you. That was what I had already gathered.

MURIEL. Mind you, she's often thought of divorcing Dad, but somehow never got round to doing it. Not that she's got a good word to say for him, mind you. She says he was the laziest, pottiest, most selfish chap she's ever come across in all her life. 'He'll come to a sticky end,' she used to say to me, when I was a little girl. 'You mark my words, Mu,' she used to say, 'if your dad doesn't end his days in jail my name's not Flossie Gosport.'

JACK. Your mother, Mrs Palmer, is plainly a remarkable prophetess. Would you and your husband mind returning to number twenty-one Upper Brecon Road as I have a rather important little matter to discuss with your dad, who will be getting in touch with you in due course.

MURIEL. Okay. Well, ta-ta for now, Dad.

ARTHUR. Ta-ta and I will arrange for three complimentary seats to be left in your name for the Thursday matinée.

TOM. Thanks a million, Dad.

ARTHUR. I'm not your dad, you know.

TOM. In law, old cock, in law.

MURIEL *and* TOM *go off.*

There is a pause, after they have gone.

EDNA (*to* ARTHUR). Darling, I must say it looks as if you've been very, very careless.

ARTHUR. Darling, there must be some hideous mistake. The whole thing is absolutely ridiculous. Jack, you must fix it.

JACK. Mr Gosport and Miss Selby – I'm afraid this is something that not even I can fix. You must face, both of you, a very unpleasant fact. You are bigamously married.

There is another pause.

ARTHUR (*calling*). Miss Fishlock!

MISS FISHLOCK (*off*). Yes, Mr Gosport.

ARTHUR. Come here a moment, would you?

MISS FISHLOCK *comes in, notebook and pencil at the ready.*

Miss Fishlock, it appears that my wife and I have committed bigamy. You'd better ring up the London Office at once and inform Mr Wilmot.

MISS FISHLOCK (*faintly*). Yes, Mr Gosport. What – did you say – you and your wife have committed?

ARTHUR. Bigamy.

MISS FISHLOCK *sways slightly and is supported by* JACK. *Then clutching her pencil firmly, she bravely writes down the fatal word – or its shorthand equivalent.*

MISS FISHLOCK. Yes, Mr Gosport.

EDNA. Silly word, isn't it? It sounds almost as if Arthur and I had committed a serious crime –

JACK. I hate to alarm you, Miss Selby, but that that is exactly what Mr Gosport has committed.

ARTHUR. You mean, I might have to pay a fine – or something like that?

JACK (*gently*). Miss Fishlock, do you happen to know the maximum penalty for bigamy?

MISS FISHLOCK *nods, biting her quivering lower lip.*

ARTHUR. What is it, Miss Fishlock?

MISS FISHLOCK (*in a whisper*). Imprisonment – for life.

There is a stunned silence.

EDNA. And – does that apply to me too, Miss Fishlock?

MISS FISHLOCK. No, Miss Selby. You haven't committed any
    crime – (*Nearly in tears.*) only Mr Gosport.

EDNA (*aghast*). They wouldn't *separate* us?

JACK. I'm afraid they would, Miss Selby.

EDNA. Oh, no, they wouldn't. They couldn't. If Arthur has to
    go to prison, I shall go too.

JACK. I doubt if that is allowed, Miss Selby. Is it, Miss
    Fishlock?

MISS FISHLOCK. No, Mr Wakefield. I don't know of any –
    prison – where – convicts – are allowed to take their wives
    with them –

*The thought is too much for her. She bursts frankly into tears
and runs into the wings.*

ARTHUR (*calling after her*). Miss Fishlock! Miss Fishlock!
    What an idiotic woman, to get so hysterical!

EDNA (*approaching him and hugging him*). Oh, my darling, I
    won't let them take you from me. I won't! I won't!

ARTHUR. Darling, there's nothing at all to get so worked up
    about. I'll make a public apology, divorce Flossie properly,
    and marry you again.

EDNA. But that would be such horrible publicity –

ARTHUR. The Arts Council will fix that. (*Suddenly galvanised
    into life.*) Now don't let's waste any more time. We've got to
    get to work.

*His eye lights on the FIRST HALBERDIER who, all this
time, has been patiently sitting in the background waiting to
be called for rehearsal.*

You! I'll do your line now. (*To* EDNA.) Darling, do you mind taking up your position in the potion scene, after you've drunk the potion.

While ARTHUR *is placing* EDNA *where he wants her for the scene,* JACK *goes up to the* FIRST HALBERDIER.

JACK. My God! How much did you hear of all that?

FIRST HALBERDIER. Oh, that's all right, Mr Wakefield, I'm not a tattle-tale. Wish me luck, Mr Wakefield. This is my great chance –

ARTHUR (*turning*). All right, Mr – Hrrhm. We're ready for you. Now, I'll give you your cue.

FIRST HALBERDIER. Thanks, Mr Gosport.

ARTHUR. Leave a five-second pause, come on, look down at the bed and see what you take to be a dead body. Now I want to get from your expression that you realise that this girl, at whose wedding you have been hired to play, has taken her own life, presumably because she couldn't face her marriage with Paris, and that she has died for love of another. Your face should express understanding of the undying conflict between spiritual love and this gross, mundane world.

FIRST HALBERDIER. Gracious!

ARTHUR. Well, if you can't do it, just look sad. Then turn and say your line to your fellow musicians who we presume to be offstage, there. (*Points.*) Understand?

FIRST HALBERDIER. Yes, Mr Gosport.

ARTHUR. All right. Go off. Jack, music.

The FIRST HALBERDIER *runs off.*

JACK. Panatrope.

ARTHUR. The heavens do lower upon us for some ill.
Move them no more by crossing their high will.

After the correct time interval, the FIRST HALBERDIER *comes on, acting hard. He gazes down at* EDNA, *and contrives to look very sad, sighing deeply and shaking his head. Then he turns slowly and faces* GEORGE CHUDLEIGH, *who has come on silently behind him.*

FIRST HALBERDIER (*simultaneously*). Faith we may put up our pipes and begone.

GEORGE (*simultaneously*). Faith we may put up our pipes and begone.

ARTHUR What? Oh Mr Hrrhm – you've come back.

GEORGE. I just felt I couldn't desert you both in the hour of your great affliction.

ARTHUR Our great affliction?

JACK. Oh, my God! How did *you* hear?

GEORGE. I was in The Feathers, and a chap in the company came in and told us all how Mr and Mrs Gosport were likely to get a life sentence for bigamy –

JACK. Oh, God! The news must be half over Brackley by now –

He runs off.

EDNA (*calling after him*). Don't worry, Jack. The company, I know, will stand by us. (*To* GEORGE.) Mr Chudleigh, it was naughty of you to leave us so suddenly, but I think I know what was the matter – we all of us suffer from an occasional *crise de nerfs*.

CHUDLEIGH. *Crise de* what!

EDNA. Nerves, Mr Chudleigh, nerves. Now come with me and I'll give you a nice strong cup of tea.

They go off together.

ARTHUR, *during this, has been staring, chin in hand, fixedly at the set. The* FIRST HALBERDIER *has been staring fixedly, and despairingly, at him.*

FIRST HALBERDIER. Mr Gosport?

ARTHUR. Yes?

FIRST HALBERDIER. Do you want me any more?

ARTHUR. What? Oh, no, thank you.

FIRST HALBERDIER. You couldn't – let me have another line to say – some time – could you?

ARTHUR (*abstractedly*). I'll keep you in mind.

FIRST HALBERDIER (*sadly*). Thanks, Mr Gosport.

> ARTHUR *goes off*. JACK *comes back*.

JACK. Too late! It's out of The Feathers and into The Green Horse, now. They've all heard it.

> JACK *wearily subsides on the stool. The* FIRST HALBERDIER *approaches him timidly*.

FIRST HALBERDIER. Mr Wakefield?

JACK. Yes?

FIRST HALBERDIER. Do you think I should give up the theatre?

JACK. Why ask me?

FIRST HALBERDIER. You know so much about life.

JACK. What has life got to do with the theatre?

FIRST HALBERDIER (*wanders to the wings*). It's an awful shame about that line. It came at such an important time, with Miss Selby and Dame Maud on, and after a pause and with a chance for face-acting. The London critics might have noticed me –

JACK (*sympathetically*). I rather doubt that. The potion scene comes very soon after the interval.

FIRST HALBERDIER. Well, cheeribye.

JACK. Cheeribye.

> *The* FIRST HALBERDIER *goes out sadly*.

JOHNNY (*off*). Mr Wakefield!

JACK (*calling*). Yes, Johnny?

JOHNNY (*off*). The lady in your dressing room says I'm to tell you time is getting on and you're not to forget your promise.

JACK (*calling*). All right. Thank you.

> *Enter* DAME MAUD.

DAME MAUD. What is this terrible news?

JACK. Oh, Dame Maud, have you been to The Feathers!

DAME MAUD. I just looked in for a little refreshment and heard this abominable slander. Jack, have some pity on an old lady and tell me it isn't true.

JACK. I'm afraid it is true, Dame Maud.

DAME MAUD. I see. Well of course I suppose you know who's at the bottom of it all, don't you?

JACK. No. Who?

DAME MAUD. The Old Vic.

JACK. Oh, I don't think so, Dame Maud.

DAME MAUD. Why dear Jack, are you quite blind? It's as clear as daylight to me. They stick at nothing, that lot, absolutely nothing. I'm going to ring them up this moment and tell them exactly what I think of them.

JACK. No, Dame Maud, you mustn't. You really mustn't.

DAME MAUD. And Sadler's Wells.

DAME MAUD goes off, followed by JACK.

The stage is empty a moment, and then a uniformed POLICEMAN walks on from the wings with firm measured tread. He looks round him. JOHNNY, still busy on the balcony, comes on.

POLICEMAN. Who's in charge here, please?

JOHNNY. Mr Wakefield. He'll be back in a minute.

After shaking the balcony once more, JOHNNY goes off. JACK comes on and stops dead at sight of the POLICEMAN.

JACK (*murmuring*). Oh God!

POLICEMAN. You Mr Wakefield?

JACK. That's right, yes. Yes, I'm Mr Wakefield, officer. Yes, that's quite correct.

POLICEMAN. I understand you want assistance.

JACK. Assistance?

POLICEMAN. One of your chaps rang up to say you were having bother at the theatre.

JACK (*infinitely relieved*). Oh, that! Oh yes. Of course, I'd forgotten. (*Laughs, rather hysterically.*) Well, well, well! Just fancy your taking all that trouble to come round here. I do think that's good of you, officer – but as a matter of fact it was all a mistake – an utter misunderstanding –

POLICEMAN. You're not having any bother?

JACK. Oh, no, no, no! No bother in the world. Not a trace of bother. Everything's quite, quite perfect.

POLICEMAN. Then I don't know what you're doing wasting our time –

JACK. Oh, my dear old chap – I can't tell you how sorry I am about that. It's awful to think of you walking all that way from the police station on a wild-goose chase. Look, sit down, my dear fellow, do. (*Brings up a stool.*) Make yourself comfortable and I'll get you a nice drink. A nice large drink. What would you like? Whisky?

The POLICEMAN *nods.*

Yes. I thought you would. Now just stay there. Don't move, will you? There are all sorts of dangerous contraptions in a theatre and you might hurt yourself and that'd be dreadful. Just sit there and relax and I'll dash and get you an enormous zonk of whisky –

He goes off, still burbling.

The POLICEMAN, *sitting patiently on the stool, is evidently rather surprised at the extreme affability of his reception. There is a pause, then* DAME MAUD *crosses the stage, another glass of Guinness clutched in her hand. She does not at first see the* POLICEMAN. *When she does she utters one single hoarse and strangled scream, and sinks slowly to the floor in a dead faint. The* POLICEMAN *rises, startled, as* JACK *comes back with a whisky.*

POLICEMAN. Here, quick! There's an old lady having a fit –

JACK. What? Oh, it's Dame Maud. Oh Lord! I suppose she saw you – I mean – she goes off at the slightest thing, you know. (*Calling.*) Johnny, Johnny! Come here, quick!

JOHNNY *comes on.*

Give me a hand with Dame Maud.

JOHNNY. Took queer, is she?

JACK. Just one of her dizzy spells –

POLICEMAN. I'd better lend a hand – I know my first aid.

JACK. Oh no. Please don't bother. You really mustn't trouble yourself, officer. It's nothing at all. She's always doing this. She's over a hundred, you know – poor old thing. Just sit down and be comfortable, and pay no attention at all.

DAME MAUD (*as she is carried off*). Get me a drink, for God's sake!

JACK *and* JOHNNY *carry her into the wings.*

The POLICEMAN *settles down once more on his stool. There is another pause and* EDNA *comes on quickly.*

EDNA. Jack – are we doing the farewell –

She sees the POLICEMAN *and stands quite motionless looking at him as he rises politely. Then, very slowly, she walks towards him.*

(*Sadly, resignedly, and melodiously.*) Ah, well. There is no purpose to be served, I suppose, in kicking against the pricks.

POLICEMAN. Beg pardon, ma'am?

EDNA. Constable – I only want to say one thing. In fifteen years my husband and I have never spent a single night apart –

POLICEMAN (*politely*). Is that so, ma'am? Just fancy!

EDNA. Not one. If we were separated, I think we would die.

POLICEMAN. Would you indeed, ma'am?

EDNA. I want you to know that nothing can keep us apart.
   Nothing; and no one – not even you, constable – can come
   between us now. If you take him, you must take me too.

POLICEMAN (*after a pause, stunned with bewilderment*).
   I see, ma'am. I'll bear that in mind.

   JACK *comes back and gasps as he sees* EDNA *with the*
   POLICEMAN.

JACK. Oh, Miss Selby, Dame Maud has been taken a bit faint.
   She's calling for you urgently.

EDNA (*tragically*). What can that matter now? I've been telling
   the constable –

JACK (*hastily*). Isn't it nice of the constable to come dashing
   round just because he heard we were having a little trouble
   in the theatre – especially when we're not having any trouble
   at all – are we?

EDNA (*understanding slowly*). Oh. Oh, I see. Constable, dear
   constable, perhaps you'd better forget what I said just now –

POLICEMAN. I'll try to, ma'am, I'm sure.

EDNA. Just a little secret between the two of us, eh? (*To*
   JACK.) What a beautiful line of the neck the constable has,
   hasn't he, Jack?

JACK. Beautiful.

POLICEMAN. Here, I say!

EDNA. Goodbye, constable, and thank you for your great, great
   kindness to us all. I shall never forget it.

   She goes off.

POLICEMAN. That was Edna Selby, wasn't it?

JACK. Yes, officer. You mustn't, you know, pay too much
   attention to anything she might have said to you. She's
   suffering from the most terrible first-night nerves.

POLICEMAN. Oh, is that the way it takes them?

JACK. Nearly always. Now, if you've quite finished your drink,
   I'd better escort you out –

POLICEMAN. Thanks. I can find my own way out –

JACK. Oh. Well, it's rather complicated and I wouldn't like you to be bothered by any of the other actors.

POLICEMAN. Are they all suffering from first-night nerves, then?

JACK. Nearly all of them. Come along, officer. I'll just clear a way for you –

He and the POLICEMAN *move to the wings.* JACK *goes out.*

The POLICEMAN *goes back for his helmet, which, in his confusion, he has left by the stool.* ARTHUR *comes in.*

ARTHUR (*explosively*). Well, really, inspector. This is too much! I do think you might have waited until after the performance.

POLICEMAN. Well – Mr Gosport, sir, I've got my work to do – you see –

ARTHUR. But, my dear inspector, you mustn't listen to a word my wife says. I can assure you we're divorced. There's no doubt at all about it.

POLICEMAN. Is that so, sir? I'd no idea.

ARTHUR. And anyway, we haven't spoken a single word to each other since the general strike.

POLICEMAN. That's too bad, sir. Your wife gave me to understand quite different –

ARTHUR. Of course she would, my dear fellow. She's out for publicity, I suppose. But I'll tell you something else, my dear chap. (*Confidentially.*) I'm not at all sure that my child is really mine –

POLICEMAN. Good gracious!

JACK *comes back in a hurry.* ARTHUR *goes up to balcony.*

JACK. My God! Mr Gosport, Miss Selby's ready for the farewell. Officer, come this way, please! Please come this way! (*Drags the* POLICEMAN *away from* ARTHUR. *In a low voice*.) You mustn't pay any attention to him either. Least of all to him.

POLICEMAN. First-night nerves too?

JACK. Far worse than that. He's completely and utterly off his rocker. It's terribly, terribly sad –

POLICEMAN. Lor' love us! But he can still act?

JACK. Yes, he can still act. That's all he can do. Come along, officer, please.

He gets him off the stage.

JOHNNY has come on to the balcony and is attaching a rope ladder to it. ARTHUR and EDNA appear on the balcony.

JOHNNY goes off, shaking his head.

ARTHUR. Give me the lighting for the farewell, please.

The light comes down to give a rosy dawn effect.

All right. Let me be ta'en, let me be put to death;
I am content, so thou wilt have it so.
I'll say yon grey is not the morning's eye,
'Tis but the pale reflex of Cynthia's brow;
Nor that is not the lark, whose notes do beat
The vaulty heaven so high above our heads:
I have more care to stay than will to go:
Come, death, and welcome! Juliet wills it so.
How is 't, my soul? Let's talk; it is not day.

EDNA. It is, it is; hie hence, be gone, away!
It is the lark that sings so out of tune
Straining harsh discords and unpleasing sharps.
Some say the lark makes sweet division;
This doth not so, for she divideth us;
Some say the lark and loathed toad change eyes;
O! Now I would they had chang'd voices too,
Since arm from arm that voice doth us affray,
Hunting thee hence with hunts-up to the day.
O! now be gone; more light and light it grows.

ARTHUR. More light and light; more dark and dark our woes.

MISS FISHLOCK suddenly flies on from the wings, and her countenance, transported with joy, is suffused with the rosy gleams of the sun now rising on Verona.

MISS FISHLOCK (*in great excitement*). Mr Gosport – Miss Selby – I know you'll forgive me for interrupting you. I have important news.

ARTHUR. Yes, Miss Fishlock?

MISS FISHLOCK. I got through to Mr Wilmot and gave him your message. He was most calm, most kind, most helpful, and most reassuring. He is coming down to Brackley tomorrow morning by an early train in person.

EDNA. How very good of him!

MISS FISHLOCK. What is more he gave me a message to pass on to you both. He says you are on no account to worry yourselves about this matter. He says he happens to know there can be no danger whatever of – of – what we feared –

ARTHUR (*triumphantly*). I knew it!

MISS FISHLOCK. He says it will probably be necessary for Miss Selby to sign a document saying that at the time she married you, Mr Gosport, she was aware that you were already married. That, of course, would have the effect of making your second marriage null and void.

ARTHUR. Oh. That's splendid!

MISS FISHLOCK. There can therefore be no question of your having committed an offence in law. Oh, Mr Gosport, he was so wonderfully brave. He went on to say that there should be little difficulty in your getting a divorce from this – this other person. Then, afterwards, should you and Miss Selby still wish it, you could get married again. Only no publicity, of course. And that, of course, would settle the entire problem once and for all. (*Beams gladly at the balcony, conscious of a duty well performed.*)

EDNA. How brilliant he is, isn't he, Arthur? I really don't know why anybody ever works for another management.

ARTHUR. Thank you, Miss Fishlock. You've done extremely well. I'm very grateful.

MISS FISHLOCK. I knew you'd both be pleased. Oh, Mr Gosport – I'm so glad – I really am. I do congratulate you. And you too, Miss Selby.

EDNA *and* ARTHUR (*murmuring*). Thank you, Miss Fishlock.

MISS FISHLOCK *goes off, again in tears, but this time, of joy.*

EDNA. Arthur, don't you think you ought to say a few words to the company? I know they'll all be overjoyed at the news.

ARTHUR Oh. Very well. (*Calling.*) Jack, assemble the company, would you?

JACK *appears.*

JACK. They're mostly in front already, Mr Gosport. (*Looking at front-of-house.*) Remain in your seats down there – everyone else on, please.

ARTHUR. Oh, right. (*To the house.*) Ladies and gentlemen. With regard to this subject of bigamy – the danger point is past. I am sure you will be delighted to hear that Mr Wilmot has discovered a way by which my marriage to Miss Selby can be rendered entirely illegal –

There is a little flutter of handclapping from the wings.

Thank you very much. Nor would it be right to let this occasion pass without extending on your behalf, on Miss Selby's and on mine, our most grateful thanks to Mr Wilmot, without whose cooperation and – ingenuity – and savoir faire – this very happy result would barely have been possible.

Another outburst of applause, louder than the first. Mr Wilmot's spies, one feels, are everywhere.

Also to Miss Fishlock, who, as usual, has had to do most of the donkey work, and has done it, as always, far better than anyone would ever expect.

One solitary clap for MISS FISHLOCK.

And lastly, ladies and gentlemen, to yourselves for the great
loyalty you have shown in this moment of crisis to my wife,
that is to say, Miss Selby, and myself. A thousand thanks.
And one other thing. I'm not a difficult man in the theatre, as
you know, but I would like to have it perfectly clear that I
consider a very great deal of time has been wasted during
this break for tea. Please see that it doesn't occur again. And
now – back to work.

ARTHUR *goes off.*

EDNA. Just a moment, everyone. I also have an announcement
to make. I know you will all be overjoyed to hear that Miss
Fishlock with characteristic ingenuity has at last successfully
completed the National Insurance forms for the entire
company.

Enter ARTHUR.

ARTHUR. Bravo. (*To* EDNA.) Let's just finish the climb down,
my dear.

EDNA. Yes.

ARTHUR *climbs onto ladder.*

Since arm from arm that voice doth us affray,
Hunting thee hence with hunts-up to the day.
O! now be gone; more light and light it grows.

ARTHUR. More light and light; more dark and dark our woes.

EDNA. Then, window, let day in, and let life out.

ARTHUR. Farewell, farewell! one kiss, and I'll descend.

He begins to climb down.

EDNA. Art thou gone so? Oh Arthur – I've just thought of
something quite, quite dreadful.

ARTHUR. What?

EDNA. Little Basil.

ARTHUR. Little Basil? (*Calling.*) Miss Fishlock!

MISS FISHLOCK *flies on again.*

MISS FISHLOCK. Yes, Mr Gosport?

ARTHUR. Ring up Mr Wilmot immediately and inform him
that he appears to have made little Basil into a little bastard –

MISS FISHLOCK. Yes, Mr Gosport.

She goes off.

ARTHUR. What's more there's far too much light on this scene
– don't you agree, dear?

EDNA. Yes, dear, I do. Especially on the balcony.

ARTHUR (*calling*). Jack!

JACK *comes on.*

There's too much from here and too much from there.
(*Waving his arms to left and right.*) Now is everyone ready?

JACK. You can't get the lights much lower than this, Mr
Gosport, or they'll go out altogether –

ARTHUR. Nonsense, my dear fellow.

The tabs draw, revealing the Verona scene with the TWO
HALBERDIERS, GEORGE CHUDLEIGH, *and* INGRAM
grouped.

Now – are we all here? I just want to do the duel.

DAME MAUD *comes onto the balcony.*

DAME MAUD. As you've stopped, dear, I thought you
wouldn't mind if I gave you another teeny little hint –

EDNA. Not just now, Auntie Maud. Do you mind? Perhaps
tomorrow –

DAME MAUD. Tomorrow will be far too late.

EDNA (*paying no attention*). There's still too much on the
balcony, Jack.

JACK (*shouting*). Bring it down more, Will! It'll never stand it,
Miss Selby.

EDNA. I'm sure it will – the lights never let us down.

ARTHUR (*in Verona*). Now, Tybalt, take the villain back again
   That late thou gav'st me; for Mercutio's soul
   Is but a little way above our heads,
   Staying for thine to keep him company;
   Either thou, or I, or both, must go with him.

INGRAM. Thou wretched boy, that didst consort him here.
   Shalt with him hence.

ARTHUR. This shall determine that.

INGRAM. What! Art thou drawn among these heartless hinds?
   Turn thee – look upon thy death!

JOYCE (*shouting above the din*). Jack! Jack! Time's up.

JACK. What? Oh, clear the stage, will you, darling? We're
   extremely busy.

JOYCE. No. I won't. Have you told them yet?

JACK. Told them what? Oh that. No, I haven't. Look, darling,
   I'm afraid you'll have to wait for me, that's all. I can't leave
   these two now. I realise that. How can I let them go behind
   the Iron Curtain without one sane man to look after them?

JOYCE. Sane? You're not sane! You're as mad as they are. This
   madhouse has infected you too.

JACK. Madhouse? This isn't a madhouse. It's just an ordinary
   dress rehearsal, that's all – now clear the stage, darling.

EDNA. Jack, dear, there's still too much light on this balcony.

JACK. If you take the lights down more than this, Miss Selby,
   they'll fuse.

EDNA. Let them fuse.

ARTHUR (*still in Verona*). Again, please. That's too quick.

JOYCE. It's no good, Jack, I'm leaving you. You'll never get
   out of this, it's bedlam, and you're in it for life. Goodbye,
   Jack, goodbye.

   She runs off the stage.

JACK. Joyce!

DAME MAUD (*looking down from the balcony*). Now that girl has talent. Who is she? Arthur – who was that girl?

ARTHUR (*still arranging the fight in Verona*). I don't know, Auntie Maud. Get her name, will you, Jack?

JACK. I've got her name, Mr Gosport. It's Joyce Langland. She was my fiancée.

ARTHUR. Good. We'll try her for *Winter's Tale* tomorrow. Now this duel is getting very sloppy. Let's go back.

EDNA. There's still too much light, Jack.

JACK. Yes, Miss Selby. Take it down more, Will. And try those thunder and lightning cues two, three, and four.

The lights suddenly go out.

My God! They've fused.

Summer lightning is now playing fitfully on the scene.

ARTHUR (*calling*). House lights. House lights.

The house lights go up. MR BURTON *rushes on.*

BURTON (*in a frantic voice*). Take those lights out! It's 7.30. There's an audience in front. Look!

He points. A row of startled faces gaze at the now visible audience, and then they scatter in panic to the wings.

The house lights go out. There is a moment's blackout, disturbed by summer lightning and a roll of thunder. Then the stage lights come on again, revealing an empty stage. ARTHUR *comes on slowly carrying his pot.*

JACK (*off, whispering frantically*). Mr Gosport! Mr Gosport! The audience is in front.

He beckons him to the wings. Other faces and other beckoning figures appear, but ARTHUR *is oblivious. He walks slowly round the pot, then, dissatisfied with its appearance, picks it up once more and walks slowly out, to the strains of the overture.*

The curtain falls.

ALL ON HER OWN

Terence Rattigan

All On Her Own was first performed on BBC2, on
25 September 1968, with the following cast:

ROSEMARY   Margaret Leighton
JOAN   Nora Gordon

Producer   Hal Burton
Designer   Stephan Paczai

The play was first performed on stage at the Overground
Theatre, Kingston, Surrey, in October 1974, with the following
cast:

ROSEMARY   Margaret Stallard

Director   Maria Riccio Bryce

The play was revived, under the title *Duologue*, in a double bill
with *The Browning Version* at the King's Head Theatre,
London, on 21 February 1976, with the following cast:

ROSEMARY HODGE   Barbara Jefford

Producer   Stewart Trotter
Designer   Geoff Stephens

Characters

ROSEMARY HODGE

Setting

Time: The present. Towards midnight.
Place: A house in Hampstead, London.

The stage is in darkness. There is the sound of a car drawing up, the engine continuing to tick over.

ROSEMARY (*unseen*).

Thank you so much. I do hope I didn't take you too far out of your way... Yes, it is rather a nice house, I have to admit. No, a little earlier. William and Mary. Far too big, of course, for these days. My late husband chose it. He was an architect, you see, and fell in love with it. Are you quite sure I can't tempt you inside for a drink? It's still quite early. Oh, is it as late as that? I quite understand. See you at the Joynson-Smythes' on Thursday, then. Goodnight. (*Calling again.*) Oh, thank you for the book. My favourite subject. I can't wait to read it.

The car drives away. Silence. Lights are suddenly switched on in an empty room which, although we may only see part of it, is plainly a large 'salon', decorated carefully according to the period. Visible to us and necessary for the action is an armchair, a sofa centre-stage, a fireplace on which is an antique pendulum clock, and a door through which ROSEMARY *has just entered. She is carrying a book which, if we can make out its title, is called* Guilt and the Human Psyche: A Study of Contemporary Literature. *She puts the book down by an armchair and pours herself a fairly hefty drink. Then she sits with it, puts it down on a table after a thirsty gulp, and picks up the book, riffling its pages quickly before throwing it down impatiently and picking up another, plainly a Crime Club selection. This too she puts down as she takes another gulp of her drink, and then stares at the sofa for a long time.*

What time did you die?

She has spoken conversationally, as if to a person sitting close to her in the room.

Gregory, what time did you die? Wasn't it about now? The police said you'd been dead between eight and nine hours, and it was eight in the morning Mrs Avon found you over there, on that sofa.

She stares at the sofa which is very tidy and clean, not looking in the least as though someone had once been found dead on it.

Or just before. Yes, it must have been before, because when she called me down the clock was striking. It's one of those silly things you remember. So it must have been about now you died.

The clock gently and musically strikes the half-hour.

A woman at a party I've just been to told me quite seriously that she talks to her husband every night at exactly the hour he died. He sends her long messages on a Ouija board or something. Well, I haven't got a Ouija board, but I'm talking to you, Gregory, and at near enough the time you died. You might just answer, you never know, and then I'll have a story to tell at a party, too. God, the party I've just been to. How you'd have hated it. *Hated* it. A young man reading a paper on Kafka and a discussion afterwards. You wouldn't even have known who Kafka was, would you?

(*In a warm, broad North Country accent.*) Kafka? Is that a new government department, love?... Oh a writer, was he? Fancy.

(*In her own voice.*) You'd have tried to steal off home before the discussion, and I wouldn't have let you, and you'd have gone off quietly to a corner of the room and got yourself quietly whistled. No, that wasn't your word.

She gets up and pours herself another drink.

Gregory, what *was* your word?

Silence.

Something revolting. Yes. You'd have got yourself quietly drunk and wouldn't have noticed my triumph in the discussion when I said to this young man: 'You see, Mr Whosit, Kafka strikes no chord on my piano. I'm afraid I don't believe in nameless fears. I believe that all fears can be named and once named can be exorcised.' Rather good. It got applause. Nice if it had been true.

She goes back to her seat.

'Are you sure you can name all your fears, Mrs Hodge?'... This was the hostess... 'Surely when you're alone at night in that great house of yours, Mrs Hodge, when your boys are away at school, you must sometimes have disquieting thoughts? I mean lonely widows usually – '

(*Sharply.*) 'Loneliness is a defeat, Mrs Ponsonby. I have far too many things to occupy my mind ever to feel lonely. I despise loneliness. I despise middle-aged women who talk to themselves at dead of night.'

She takes a long drink.

But I'm not talking to myself. I'm talking to you, Gregory, aren't I? Talking to a dead you.

She laughs.

Well, talking to a live you wasn't very different. It was still talking to myself. I hope you didn't hear that because it was rude and I was never rude to you in all our married life, was I? Unfailingly polite – wasn't it 'unfailingly' you used to say, or 'invariably'?… No. 'Unfailingly.' Poor Gregory – how you hated that, didn't you? How you longed for just one honest, vulgar, hammer-and-tongs, husband-and-wifely flamer! But I never gave it to you, did I? I was brought up to be polite, you see – unfailingly polite. Was that so wrong?

(*Answering herself.*) Yes, it was. It was pretty damn bloody!

(*Surprised.*) Do you know – talking to you is rather good for me, Gregory. I should do it more often. It might even make me honest.

She takes another sip of her drink, then again looks over at the sofa.

I called you an architect again tonight, Gregory. I even said it was you who chose this house. That's a laugh considering how you hated it. I call you an architect all the time, now that you're no longer there to deny it.

(*In Gregory's North Country accent.*) Why do you call me what I never was, Rosemary, and never could have been? You make me feel as if I'd wasted all my life. I was a builder and proud of it. I despise bloody architects. They're always so busy concealing lavatory pipes they forget they've got to flush.

(*In her own voice*.) Yes. You beat me on that, Gregory. The only
real battle I suppose you ever won. To stop you talking about
lavatories all over Hampstead, and making people think I was
married to a plumber, we settled on 'builder'. Well, 'building
contractor'. It sounded better.

She goes to get another drink.

All right. I'm being honest with you, Gregory. Now you be
honest with me.

Drink in hand, she stands over the sofa looking down at it.

Tell me if the police and the coroner and the insurance people
were right when they said it was a drunken accident? Or if I'm
right now when I say you killed yourself?

Silence. ROSEMARY, *as if consciously committing a
blasphemous act, stretches herself out on the sofa.*

(*In his accent*.) But Rosemary, darling, why should I kill myself?
I had everything to live for, hadn't I? I'd just sold my business in
Huddersfield for a lot of money, and bought a beautiful house in
Hampstead, and for the first time in my life could enjoy all the
ease and comfort of a charming, civilised, cultured retirement in
London, with my charming, civilised, cultured wife beside me,
and my two charming, civilised, cultured sons at Eton. And my
wife is still quite young, you know, as wives go, and still quite
attractive in her way – well, I find her so anyway, but I suppose
you'd say I was prejudiced about that and always have been. Oh,
yes. I was a lucky man when I was alive. There's no doubt about
it. Why on earth should I have killed myself?

She gets up from the sofa and goes back to her chair.

(*In her own voice*.) If I answered that for you, Gregory, would
you still tell me whether you did?

After a pause.

Of course you wouldn't.

(*In Gregory's voice*.) But all that happened that night, Rosemary
darling, was that after we had that little tiff about whether I
couldn't go out on the town with Alf Fairlie from the rugger
club instead of going with you to the ballet – which I never did

fancy very much, as you know – along with the Fergusons who always treated me like some kind of nit who'd married a mile above myself. Not the only ones to do that, down here in Hampstead, come to that, which doesn't always seem to put you out too much, Rosemary love – be honest now, does it? Is that why we're in Hampstead? Is it – to show me my place?

(*Stridently, in her own voice.*) Oh, my God! That wasn't me. I'm not as honest as that, am I? Gregory, that must have been you! Gregory, are you in this room?

(*Looking around anxiously.*) Are you in this room, Gregory?

(*More loudly.*) Are you?

There is no answer and no sign. ROSEMARY *swallows her drink and pours another.*

Let's try again!

(*In North Country accent again.*) Well, we had this little argie-bargie, love – remember? And afterwards, you went up to bed – never a cross word, mind you – impeccably polite as.

(*In her own voice, excitement mounting.*) It was 'impeccably', not 'unfailingly' or 'invariably'. No, it wasn't – it wasn't – but it *was* just then. Gregory, you *are* here! You are, aren't you? You're here, with me, in this room?

Again there is no answer and no sign.

(*Controlling herself.*) Go on. Go on, Gregory!

She begins to speak again, with a conscious imitation of his accent, carefully contrived at first – as in the two previous 'Gregory' speeches – and only later does her voice quite suddenly seem to become a spontaneous expression of a living personality.

All right, Rosemary darling, it was like this. You went up to bed, see, impeccably polite.

(*In her own voice.*) That was me that time, not you!

(*In his voice.*) ... as always, and it was early still – not more than nine o'clock or thereabouts, and so I'm afraid, love, I got myself at that decanter that you're holding now.

(*Very gently.*) Going my way, are you, love?

ROSEMARY *slams the decanter down as if she had hardly known she had it in her hand.*

Careful of the whiskey, love. It's bad stuff for widows living on their own. You had two before you went to the party. Not many there, I shouldn't think, knowing those parties – had Algerian burgundy, I expect – but you probably sneaked yourself an extra glass or so, shouldn't be surprised. And now three since eleven twenty-five.

ROSEMARY *pours some of her drink back into the decanter.*

That's better, Rosemary darling. Can't be too careful, I always say. Look what happened to me that night.

ROSEMARY, *with an effort at control, pours water into her drink and then, as if shrugging off Gregory's presence, deliberately adds to it from the decanter.*

(*Still in Gregory's voice.*) Think it's not me talking to you? Think it's just you talking to yourself?

(*In her own voice.*) I know it's just me talking to myself – in a bad Huddersfield accent.

(*In his voice.*) I didn't talk in a Huddersfield accent, love. I was born in Newcastle.

(*Sharply, in her own voice.*) Did I know that? Yes, of course, I must have.

(*Controlled.*) All right, Gregory. What happened to you that night? Tell me.

There is a pause, as if she really were expecting a reply. Then, she laughs.

Of course! The game is – I begin and then you take over.

(*In his voice.*) Well, Rosemary darling, you'd gone to bed, as I told you, and I got at the decanter and got myself fairly whistled.

(*In her own voice.*) No, 'whoozled'. That was your word. You got yourself '*whoozled*'.

(*Unconsciously, in his voice*.) Aren't you going to say 'I wish you wouldn't use that *awful* expression, Gregory! If you mean "drunk", why don't you say "drunk"?'

(*In her own voice, now stiff with fear*.) Because you weren't drunk. When you came up to my room you were quite sober. If you hadn't been, I'd have smelled it on your breath. I'd had enough experience of it these last fifteen years.

(*In his voice*.) But not much these last ten years, eh, love? Not from very close. And not at all that night.

(*In her voice*.) You said you wanted to sleep down here. And I told you to please yourself.

(*In his voice*.) Aye, you did. And I pleased myself. It was then, if you want to know, that I got myself really whoozled. Boy, did I get whoozled!

(*After a pause; in her own voice*.) You expected to come to bed?

(*In his voice*.) Not expected. Hoped, you might say. I'd said I was sorry, hadn't I?

ROSEMARY *nods*.

And it was a Friday night, after all. I know it wasn't back at Huddersfield, not working on Saturday and all – not working *any* bloody day down here! And I know things like that had, well – lapsed a bit lately between us – but, well, it's always a good way to make up a quarrel, isn't it?

ROSEMARY *nods again*.

Don't cry, love. There's no need for that now. I told you, I didn't expect. I only hoped.

(*After a long pause; in her own voice*.) What about those pills?

(*In his voice*.) Well, this sofa isn't much of a place to sleep on, you know. A man my size.

ROSEMARY*'s gaze is fixed on the sofa*.

Oh, very aesthetical, and quite the rage in North London, I don't doubt, but not too comfy for a man in a bit of a state. Whoozled, I know, but still in quite a state what with one thing and another. So I went up to the bathroom –

The immediate impression is that ROSEMARY *is listening intently, although of course she continues to speak.*

– and I found that bottle of pills that you use. Nembutal or some such name. Little yellow things. And I gave myself enough to make myself sleep – just two or three.

(*Interrupting herself; quietly.*) Six.

(*After a pause; in his voice.*) Was it six? I told you I was whoozled, didn't I? Well, doesn't that show it was an accident, love? I mean, if I'd wanted to kill myself I'd have taken sixteen, wouldn't I?

There is a pause. Then ROSEMARY *finishes her drink and shrugs hopelessly.*

(*In her own voice.*) Not if you wanted me to think it *was* an accident. And to let me have the money from the insurance.

(*With a sudden access of real grief.*) Oh, my God, do you think that money could make up for you? Oh, you bloody, bloody fool!

A moment.

But how were you to know?

She goes to replenish her drink.

Yes! Another whiskey. It'll be the last. Oh, Gregory, why did you do it? It's silly to ask you that, isn't it? I know why you did it – if you did it. Did you? No, what's the point! It'll only be my own brain answering for you again, and my brain will go on thinking no, and believing yes – yes and no, no and – until the end of time.

After taking a gulp of her drink.

And when will that be, Gregory? Are you allowed to know these things? And would you tell me if you were?

A moment.

No, you'd never say anything to hurt me, would you?

She looks round the room in silence for a moment.

It doesn't matter. Yes, I'm lonely, Gregory, and I do miss you. Quite terribly I miss you. Does that surprise you? I expect it does. It certainly surprised me.

She finishes her drink.

So you had everything to live for, did you? Your work, which you loved, finished by me. All your friends lost, and your life uprooted – by me. Your children, whom you loved, and who could have loved you, made to despise you – by me. And a wife – 'unfailingly polite' – who only knew she loved you when you were dead. And whom you loved and went on loving in spite of – I can say it. Oh yes, I'm brave enough! In spite of her driving you to your death.

(*Raising her voice for the first time.*) I did, Gregory, didn't I? I want the real truth now, and I'm not going to answer for you any longer through my brain and with my voice! You'll have to find some other way. Open a door, break a window, upset a table! Make some sign! But do something, and tell me the real truth! Did I kill you?

Nothing stirs in the room and there is no sound.

I killed you, didn't I? Say it, Gregory – say it!

The clock quietly and musically begins to strike midnight. There is no other sound. ROSEMARY *waits until it is finished, then goes quietly round the room, turning off the lights. The last light left burning is by the sofa. Just before she turns it off, she gently puts her hand on the part where Gregory's head might, one night, have lain. Then she looks round and sees the decanter still half-full. After the briefest hesitation she picks it up and takes it with her as she turns off the light and goes out. A light seems to linger on the sofa before final complete and silent darkness.*

Curtain.

The End.